Judy Martin's Ultimate Rotary Cutting Reference

CROSLEY-GRIFFITH PUBLISHING COMPANY, INC.
Grinnell, Iowa

CONTENTS

ACKNOWLEDGMENTS: Special thanks to Jean Nolte, Phil Moore, and Steve Bennett for proofreading tirelessly and to Chris Hulin for her feedback all through the project.

Written and illustrated by Judy Martin
Photography by Steve O'Connor, O'Connor Photography, Grinnell, Iowa
Printed in the United States of America

ISBN 0-929589-04-1
Published by Crosley-Griffith Publishing Company, Inc.
1321 Broad Street, Grinnell, Iowa 50112
(515) 236-4854 phone or fax
e-mail crosgriff@aol.com
First Printing 1997
15 14 13 12 11 10 9 8 7 6 5 4 3 2

INTRODUCTION & IMPORTANT NOTES

At last, rotary cutting is discussed in complete detail to help beginners and advanced quilters alike. *Judy Martin's Ultimate Rotary Cutting Reference* will answer any question you might have about rotary cutting, from the most basic questions about tools and their use to advanced questions about the most up-to-date shortcuts.

ALL THE ANSWERS

Do you cut patches that don't fit together? Learn how to cut perfect, accurate patches the first time, every time. Do you have the right tools for the job? Find out the best tools for a basic tool kit, and what you will want to add if you plan to do lots of rotary cutting. Does your ruler slip? Discover four ways of preventing this problem.

Are you afraid of the bias? Learn five secrets to help you master it. Do you know the best sizes to rotary cut octagons and star blocks? Find the answers here. Do you wish you didn't have to do the math every time you cut a shape? Find easy charts with seam allowances already added to the cutting dimensions for each patch.

Do you waste time and fabric using so-called "shortcuts" that are nothing more than detours? Find out how various methods compare so that you can choose the best method for you. Are you ready to go beyond the basics to refine your rotary cutting and expand your pattern possibilities? Learn to cut shapes you've never cut before, and learn tricks for cutting faster, more accurately, and more efficiently than ever.

HELPFUL DETAILS

Most of the information in this book has never before been published. For the first time, you will find specific rotary cutting details for an amazing variety of patch shapes and sizes. Step-by-step, illustrated instructions show you at a glance how to cut any shape. Helpful charts list finished patch dimensions and cut sizes with seam allowances already figured. You will even find yardage information for each patch. Learn to rotary cut shapes you never thought you could, often using just your regular ruler.

The first part of the book covers general procedures, tools, and specific techniques. Common problems are addressed in a question-and-answer format.

The last part of the book offers charts, directions, and illustrations for rotary cutting a wide variety of

shapes in a range of useful sizes. Before you begin cutting, be sure to read pages 24 and 25. The chart introductions and directions also include some details you won't want to miss.

With the help of this book, you'll soon be cutting like a pro with no more than a quick glance at the chart. You will refer to this book so often, you will wonder how you ever got along without it.

DON'T MISS THESE TOPICS

This book includes basic rotary cutting information to help beginners. More experienced quiltmakers may be tempted to jump right into using the charts without reading the text. Please don't start cutting without at least giving the book one quick run through. You'll be glad you took the time to look over the material. It is full of helpful tidbits for quiltmakers who already know rotary cutting. Subheads in bold will help you key into topics that interest you.

New Techniques. Many new rotary cutting applications are introduced in this book. Eleven specific techniques are discussed in detail on pages 13–16. At least half of them are probably new to you. Be sure to read about these new techniques:

    1. cut lengthwise strips
    2. trim a triangle
    3. trim 2 triangles
    4. S45 subcuts
    5. cut 2:1 angles
    6. fold & trim

These techniques are possibly new to you as well:

    7. right angle subcuts
    8. cut parallel to the diagonal

New Perspectives. This book takes a sensible approach to rotary cutting, offering a few improvements to common cutting practices. The Comparison of Methods on pages 9–12 will open your eyes to the pros and cons of various shortcuts.

The chapter, What Patch Do I Need?, beginning on page 22, provides exciting new information about the best sizes for making LeMoyne Stars, octagons, diagonal squares, and more. I call these special sizes "Magic Measures." Designers: don't miss this section.

The questions and answers beginning on page 19 offer something for everyone. You will learn the secrets to professional results here.

I know that you are anxious to explore *Judy Martin's Ultimate Rotary Cutting Reference* and the world of rotary cutting, so let's get going.

ROTARY CUTTING TOOLS

BASIC ROTARY CUTTING TOOLS
You'll need just three tools to start rotary cutting:
1. a rotary cutter and extra blades
2. a cutting mat
3. a long, wide rotary ruler

Features to look for in basic tools are described below. I get into some of the advantages and disadvantages of various brands. I will leave it up to you to weigh these, considering your personal circumstances, and decide what is best for you.

When you are ready to get serious about rotary cutting, you will want to add a few tools, as described in the Deluxe Tool Kit section on page 7.

The Rotary Cutter
The rotary cutter looks like a pizza cutter, with a wheel blade attached to a handle. However, it is razor-sharp. Look for a comfortable handle, an easy rolling action, and a retractable shield to cover the blade when it is not in use.

Blades. Cutters are available with small, medium, or large blades, measuring 28, 45, 60, or 65 millimeters in diameter. Most make straight cuts, although wavy blades are available, as well. For patchwork, use a straight blade. A large blade makes easy work of long, straight cuts clear across the fabric. A smaller blade can be maneuvered around curves and is easier to start and stop with some precision. The new Softouch® cutter from Fiskars® is convertible for use with medium or large blades. Most quilters are well served by a large or medium cutting blade.

Every blade I have encountered claims to be interchangeable with same-size blades of other brands. Some blades hold their edge longer than others, and some are too sharp and can damage your mat. I have used Olfa® blades for years, and I prefer them to other blades I have tried. If you are dissatisfied with the sharpness or durability of a particular blade, try another brand.

Handle Design. Some cutters, such as the ones from Fiskars®, have curved, ergonomically designed handles. These may offer more comfort to individuals who cut for hours on end or who have arthritis or carpal tunnel problems. These conditions may be aggravated by gripping and applying pressure with a rotary cutter. I'm healthy, but I sometimes cut for hours on end. I have been completely satisfied with my straight-handled Olfa® cutter. I particularly like Olfa's® newer models with improved handles. I have recently tried the new Fiskars® Softouch®, with its curved and cushioned handle. It feels very comfortable to me, and I plan to test it thoroughly soon.

Safety. The Fiskars® Softouch® has a secure, easy-to-use blade guard mechanism with a spring action. This is my favorite guard for adult use, although I suspect the bright orange blade-lowering button may be tempting to children. (Of course, there is no substitute for keeping your cutter and extra blades out of reach of children.) The Quilter's Rule™ has the most secure blade guard that I have seen. It should foil most children. It is also slightly harder for the adult to release. The Olfa® cutter's blade guard is easy to use, but it can slip out of place if the blade screw works loose. Of course, I recommend that you keep the screw properly tightened for safety as well as better cutting action.

Always exercise caution when using a rotary cutter. Use the blade guard when you are not cutting. If you talk with your hands, for goodness sake, put your cutter down before you open your mouth. Keep your fingers well clear of the edge of the ruler when cutting. And, finally, cut from side to side or away from your body, rather than toward it.

Care and Feeding. Keep your cutting area clear of papers, pins, and other materials that might be ruined or might damage your blade. According to Judy Martin's Law, anything on your cutting mat will invariably jump into the path of your blade. Running over pins is a definite no-no. Cutting through pizzas and their boxes is also not advised.

Change blades as soon as you notice a nick or signs of dullness, such as missed threads, gaps in the cutting line, or the need to apply excess pressure. Excess pressure may be hard on your mat, as well as your wrist, so keep your blade sharp. Be sure to pay attention to the proper placement of the blade, washer (if any), screw, and nut when you change the blade. Always replace your blade with the size of blade specified for your cutter. Blades may be sharpened if they are not badly nicked. Some manufacturers discourage sharpening blades yourself, suggesting that you find a qualified expert to sharpen them.

The Cutting Mat
The cutting mat provides a tough work surface that not only protects your table from the blade, it also preserves the blade and makes the cutting easier. The mat should have a surface that holds the fabric in place. Its color should contrast with your fabrics. I have been pleased with both my Olfa® Rotary Mat and my Omnimat®. The Omnimat® is a brighter

green that contrasts better with the colors I tend to use. On the other hand, I find the Olfa® mat a bit better at letting me cut clear through the bottom layer of stacked fabric when my blade is getting dull. (Of course, I don't recommend using a dull blade.)

Self-Healing. In my opinion, the self-healing mats are best. Several manufacturers, including Olfa® and Omnigrid®, make them. As you cut your fabric, the cuts in the mat naturally close, leaving little or no scarring of the surface. Some other mats do not heal and may scar deeply. Such a mat came with my cutting table, and the mat has been rendered useless in places. Most mats eventually have surface scratches, but these should not interfere with your cutting. (If your mat is scratched or grooved deeply, you need to replace your mat or your cutting will suffer.)

Size. Your cutting mat should be large enough to accommodate your usual strip sizes. Your rotary cutting will be more efficient if you keep your strips and patches in place, rather than handling them unnecessarily. For this reason, a long, narrow mat or a small square mat may be impractical for home use. (You may like them for travel use.) I recommend a mat at least 18" by 24" in size for everyday use. My personal choice is a table-sized mat.

Color. The mat should be a color that contrasts with your ruler's lines and/or your fabrics. I have seen bright green, light gray, dark gray, and white mats. The Omnimats® are bright green on the front and light gray on the back, offering contrast against any color.

The Myth of Mat Rulings. Most mats have a grid of one-inch squares printed on them with measurements around the edges. This may be occasionally useful for cutting very wide strips or extra-large patches for which you don't have a suitable ruler. However, most of the time you are better off ignoring the mat's rule lines. The reason is simple: using the mat's rulings doubles your work. In order to use the mat's lines, you must carefully align the fabric with the mat. Then you must also align the ruler with the mat. It is easier to simply plop down your fabric with no regard to the mat's rulings, and align your ruler with the fabric. Some quilters turn their mats over to avoid the distraction of the printed mat rulings.

Care and Feeding. Cutting mats can warp and ripple when exposed to heat. Don't leave them in a hot car, and don't even think about ironing on them. Store them flat when not in use.

The Rotary Ruler

Your rotary ruler should be thick (about ⅛"), clear plastic, printed on the underside. Fine, crisp lines improve your accuracy, and dashed lines help you see the edge of your fabric under the line. Don't trust a ruler if its lines are clearly not parallel or perpendicular to the edges of the plastic.

Ruler Length. Your basic rotary ruler should be as small as possible and as big as necessary to cut the strips you desire. The shorter a ruler is, the more maneuverable it will be. However, your ruler needs to be a little longer than your strips. If you cut crosswise strips through fabric folded in half, you will need a 24"-long ruler. If you cut crosswise strips through fabric folded in fourths, a 12"-long ruler will suffice. If you cut lengthwise strips from half yards or fat quarters, as I do, a 19" ruler is perfect. Choose a ruler length to accommodate your cutting methods.

Ruler Width. Wider rulers let you cut strips for bigger patches, but narrower rulers are lighter and more maneuverable. If you have just one ruler, make it wide enough to cut most of the strips you will need. Usually something in the 6" to 8" range is ideal. I seldom need strips bigger than 6⅞". Look at the strip widths in this book, to find sizes that you might expect to cut with some frequency. The Master Piece® 45 is an 8" x 24" ruler, and Judy Martin's Rotaruler 16 is 7" x 19". Quilter's Rule™ makes a 6½" x 24" ruler, and Omnigrid® makes one 6" x 24".

Two rulers may be used together to add up to a sufficient strip width. It is worth investing in a wider ruler if this situation comes up often, but for the occasional wide patch, two rulers will serve just fine. Rulers that end in a fraction can be confusing to add together. Patched Works, Inc. came up with a tidy solution to this in the Rotary Mate, 3½" x 12", and the Big Mama, 6½" x 12". When either of these rulers is paired with the 3½" x 24" Rotary Rule, the numbering along the right side is continuous, so you won't need to add the two rulers' numbers together.

Alternate blocks and edge triangles may be too big to cut from strips using your basic ruler or even using two rulers together. See the "Big Square Ruler" section on page 7 for help with these. Usually these setting pieces are not needed in huge quantities, and they can be rotary cut one at a time.

I recommend a ruler 6" to 8" wide if you have just one ruler. If you don't already have a long, wide ruler, get one now. A ruler 3" or 4" wide is handy for smaller strips and patches, so you may want to have one of these, as well. However, small strips and patches can be cut using your wider ruler, so there are some other tools that I would recommend before you invest in a long, narrow ruler. (See the Deluxe Tool Kit section, page 7.)

Rulings. Some rulers have a minumum of rule lines; others have a complete grid of ⅛" squares. It is easier to follow your chosen rule line if there are few lines on the ruler. However, with few lines, you may find that the ruler lacks lines to follow for some of your most common strip sizes, such as the 2⅞" strip needed to cut 2" finished triangles. The most common patch sizes require strips cut 1½", 1⅞", 2½", 2⅞", 3¼", 3½", 3⅞", 4¼", 4½", 4⅞", 5¼", 6½", or 6⅞" wide. A practical ruler should have lengthwise lines for any size you want to cut.

Many rulers have lengthwise rulings at ¼" intervals, often with tick marks for eighths. These rulers are less cluttered than more finely ruled ones. However, they won't have lines for some of the common strip sizes. It is easier to cut strips following a line than it is to cut them following tick marks spaced an inch or more apart.

The Rotary Rule, Rotary Mate and Big Mama from Patched Works, Inc. provide a good compromise. These rulers have lines for the inches, halves, and quarters, as well as the most commonly used eighths. They skip the other eighths. They are readable and practical for the most common patch shapes and sizes.

I personally like a grid of ⅛" squares on a ruler. Such a grid lets you cut the common shapes and sizes as well as the more exotic shapes and the useful Magic Measure sizes described on page 22. The ⅛" grid also helps you align two sides to square up a strip or patch anywhere on the ruler. Omnigrid's® 3" x 18" model 18G is a good example, as is the 8" x 24" Master Piece® 45. Judy Martin's Rotaruler 16 offers a ⅛" grid with the further advantage of rulings that vary in line width and dash length to make it easy to find and follow the appropriate fraction. At a glance, this ruler appears to have a lot of lines. However, in actual use, it is supremely readable.

Ink Colors. Rulers are available printed in black, pink, metallic gold, black-and-yellow, black-and-orange, or white. Each aims to provide the best contrast against a variety of fabric colors. (In the case of white, it is meant as a supplement to a black ruler.)

I have difficulty focusing on bright colors. Perhaps it has something to do with my astigmatism. I prefer black rulings against most fabrics. Even on dark fabrics, following a line is easy enough, as it will contrast with the mat. Black numbers can be hard to read on dark fabric, though. You will have no problem finding the correctly numbered rule line if you flag it as described on pages 19–20.

If you don't mind investing in a second ruler, Patched Works, Inc. has a perfect solution to the contrast problem. All three of their rulers are available in a choice of black or white ink.

If the bright color works for you, Omnigrid's® black-and-yellow rule lines offer good contrast on

most fabrics. I prefer the models, such as 18G and 4G, with more black lines than yellow ones. Omnigrid's® black-on-yellow numbers have their own contrasting background for readability on any color and on even the busiest prints.

Angles. Your basic ruler should have a 45° angle printed on it. All of the rulers I have mentioned in this chapter have a 45° angle. Some rulers have 60° and possibly 30° angles, as well. These angles are not needed for most patchwork, but you may want them for such special applications as hexagons, equilateral triangles, and related patches.

Optional Features. Beginners may find it difficult to prevent the ruler from slipping as they cut, although most quilters soon get the knack of walking their hand down the ruler to steady it. Quiltmakers who continue to have trouble, as well as beginners, may like the Quilter's Rule™, with its raised lines that offer some gripping action against the fabric. You may find this to be just the ticket. I used one as a beginner in rotary cutting and liked it very much then. The Quilter's Rule™, with its gripping action comes in 6½" x 24", 4½" x 14", and 6½" x 6½" sizes as well as in specialty triangles. If you are not having trouble with ruler slippage, choose a ruler based on its size, rulings and ink colors, rather than on its gripping qualities.

You can get a ruler having a lip that hugs the edge of the table. If your table is straight and true, you can make parallel cuts by sliding the lip of the ruler down the table. You still need to align the fabric with the ruler for the first cut and align the proper ruling with the fabric for each successive cut, so I am not convinced that there is a big advantage here. I find it easier to align a ruler *over* the fabric than to align fabric *under* a fixed ruler, so I prefer a regular ruler to one with a lip.

Safety. Short of getting bopped on the head or poked in the eye with it, a ruler probably isn't going to injure anyone. It is the rotary cutter that you need to be careful about. Always keep your fingers clear of the edge of the ruler when you cut. I have never had the cutter jump over the edge of the ruler and threaten my fingers. However, if you worry about your rotary cutter "derailing" in this way, you can get a safety shield to affix to the edge of your ruler to protect your fingers.

Care and Feeding. Rotary rulers are generally pretty sturdy and stand up to most of what you subject them to. They may ding or break when they are dropped. I know from experience that a ruler can break in half when your toddler uses it as a walking bridge between your chair and ottoman. Don't throw them (the rulers or the toddlers) around casually.

Rulers can also be damaged by an errant blade, so watch where you aim your cutter. Ink can rub off after much use or a little abuse. If you tape anything to your ruler, be sure to tape it to the top surface so you don't damage the printing. (You can use it face down.) Plastic is a material that shrinks and stretches in response to temperature changes. You don't want your inches to change size from one day to the next, so keep your ruler out of extreme heat or cold. Don't leave it in a hot car, for example. Treated with care, your ruler can serve you for a good, long time.

THE DELUXE TOOL KIT

The basic tools will get you through most rotary cutting tasks. A handful of additional tools will make a difference in how quickly and easily you accomplish these tasks. They will also help you refine your cutting and tackle a broad range of patch shapes and sizes. A deluxe tool kit should start with the three basic tools and add the items numbered 4–8, as described here.

Basic Tool Kit:
  1. a rotary cutter and extra blades
  2. a cutting mat
  3. a long, wide rotary ruler

Add for Deluxe Tool Kit:
  4. a big square ruler
  5. a small ruler
  6. a Shapemaker 45 ruler
  7. a Point Trimmer
  8. a long, narrow ruler (optional)

The features discussed in the Basic Rotary Tools section apply to the deluxe tools, as well. You may also want a few of the Specialty Tools described in the next section.

The Big Square Ruler. Your basic ruler won't be big enough for cutting some alternate blocks, sashes, edge triangles, and other big patches that your quilts may call for. Sometimes, two rulers together are still not wide enough. Invest in a big square ruler for these situations. Big squares are available in 8", 12", 12½", 15" and 16" sizes. I prefer the larger ones.

The Small Ruler. You will need your basic, long ruler to cut strips, and it will serve for subcutting strips into patches, as well. However, for these short subcuts, a 4" to 6" square ruler such as the Omnigrid® 4G or 6G or the Quilter's Rule™ QR-MS is surprisingly handy. A small rectangle such as Quilter's Rule's™ 4½" x 14" model QR-JR or Patched Works' 6½" x 12" Big Mama can also be useful. Unless you are terribly serious about getting your exercise, stop hefting your basic, big ruler for the little jobs. A little ruler will take a big chunk out of the time you spend on the little cutting jobs.

The Shapemaker 45 Ruler. This multipurpose ruler from Judy Martin's Ultimate Rotary Tools lets you easily cut prisms, trapezoids, triangles, octagons, Snowballs, and Bow Ties. It cuts right triangles with the long side on the straight grain as well as those with the short sides on the straight grain. It also cuts right triangles from the same strips that you use to cut squares. It cuts shapes in a complete range of sizes, not just the common ones. The tool offers an easy, efficient way to cut many shapes and the *only* way to cut others. A glance at the rotary cutting charts in this book should convince you of the indispensability and versatility of the S45.

The Point Trimmer. Trimming points minimizes show-through and excess bulk in the seam allowances. Trimming points *before you sew* saves time by letting you cut through several layers. More importantly, pretrimmed points improve your machine piecing by helping you align patches perfectly for stitching. The fastest, easiest way to pretrim points is using the Point Trimmer from Judy Martin's Ultimate Rotary Tools. This tool lets you trim off the excess seam allowance at any 45° point. Use it for trapezoids, triangles, parallelograms, and diamonds of any size. Three different trims are included for perfect alignment in any 45° situation. Save time by trimming four stacked patches at once. Pretrim each stack of patches immediately after cutting it, before the stack gets jostled with handling. The little bit of time and effort you take in pretrimming points will be well rewarded. You will be amazed at your improved precision and ease of sewing.

The Long, Narrow Ruler. Many quilters start out with a long, narrow ruler. I prefer a long, *wide* ruler for the basic tool kit, but there are times when you will be glad you have the narrower one, as well. If your basic ruler is 6" to 8" wide, a supplemental narrower ruler may not be a top priority. Still, a long, narrow ruler does come in handy for small strips and patches. Of course, you can cut these with your long, wide ruler, but if you do a lot of cutting, you will enjoy the ease of handling a smaller ruler when the patch size allows it. Consider the 3½" x 24" Rotary Rule from Patched Works, Inc. or the 3" x 18" model 18G from Omnigrid®.

OTHER TOOLS

A wide range of specialty tools and templates is available to help you rotary cut. On pages 17–18, I discuss a sampling of these tools and give instructions for using some of the multipurpose ones. However, before I discuss such specialized material, it is important that you have a good understanding of rotary cutting methods.

ROTARY CUTTING BASICS

PREPARATIONS FOR PERFECT CUTTING

A few little preparations before you cut will make a huge difference in your quilts.

Check the seam gauge. An inaccurate seam gauge is the most common cause of patchwork sewing problems. Don't simply assume that your presser foot is ¼" wide. Stitch a seam, then measure the distance from the stitching line to the raw edges. If you discover that your presser foot is wider than you thought, invest in a new foot or affix a strip of masking tape to your throat plate as a guide. (If your feed dogs are in the path of the tape, run the tape from the front of the machine up to the feed dogs, without taping over them.)

Test the pattern. Some of the cutting measurements in this book are perfect; others are rounded off slightly to a measurable number. For example, my chart lists 2⅞" as the cutting size for right triangles that finish 2". This figure is slightly rounded. It is also used universally and works beautifully.

Quiltmakers who want to adjust for takeup (see page 19), for rounding, or for their own sewing should cut and sew a test block first. Adjustments can be made by adding or subtracting a thread when you cut the patches for the rest of the quilt. Instead of centering the rule line exactly over the cut edge of the fabric, as usual, you can add a thread by aligning the rule line one thread inside the cut edge of the fabric. To subtract a thread you simply align the ruling one thread's width beyond the edge of the fabric.

Prepare the fabrics before you cut. Prepare fabrics by testing for colorfastness and preshrinking, if desired. Now is your last chance to iron *every* wrinkle out of your fabric. Use steam if you like, or leave the fabric a little damp and use a dry iron.

Iron the Layers. Cutting through four layers of unfolded fabric maximizes speed with suitable accuracy. To keep the layers evenly stacked, iron the fabrics separately, then *together* with a dry iron. Add one fabric at a time and iron the layers together after each addition. Let the fabric cool briefly before transferring the stack to the cutting mat.

CUTTING BASICS

Here are some basics that apply to all methods.

Trim the selvedges. Selvedges do not belong in patchwork. The tighter weave, holes, and writing along the selvedges can be deeper than the usual ¼" seam allowances. Some fabrics are noticeably tighter in the selvedge, making them billow just beyond the selvedge. Trim these before layering fabrics or cutting

them. Otherwise, press and layer four fabrics to trim their selvedges all at once. Simply place the ⅜" rule line (or another more suitable ruling) along the selvedge and cut along the ruler's edge.

Make a clean cut. Even if a fabric has a cleanly cut edge, shave off a little through all layers after stacking fabrics to ensure perfectly even strips.

Measuring. Simply center the desired line of the ruler exactly over the clean edge of the fabric and cut along the ruler's edge.

The cutting stroke. To rotary cut a strip or patch, run your rotary blade along the top edge of the ruler or the side of the ruler. (Never try to cut along the bottom edge of the ruler.) Right handers cut from right to left along the top or away from their body along the ruler's right side. Hold the ruler with one hand while you operate the rotary cutter with the other. You need to hold the ruler firmly as you cut. To keep the ruler from slipping, change your grip to steady the ruler alongside the blade. Move your hand down the length of the ruler as you cut. Simply stop and hold the cutter in place while you move your ruler hand. Be sure to keep your fingers clear of the edge, as the blade is dangerously sharp. The blade should be straight up and down (not tilted) and directly against the ruler. It helps to roll the blade away from the center at the ends of the strip, so start by rolling backwards from an inch or so in from the end. Then roll it forward to the opposite end.

Left-Handed Rotary Cutting. The cutting *directions* in this book are for right handers and left handers alike. The *illustrations* show the right-handed version. The lengthwise strips shown are cut the same way for everyone, with a stroke along the top edge of the ruler. For subcuts, left handers cut along the left edge of the ruler. Here are a few additional guidelines for left handers:

1. Left handers clean up the right end of the strip and start cutting there.

2. For parallel angled cuts, left handers trim off the *bottom right* corner of the strip and make parallel subcuts from there. When right handers trim off the top left corner, left handers trim off the *top right* corner of the strip.

3. Cutting from the opposite end of the strip, as left handers do, reverses asymmetrical patches. For mirror images in equal numbers from folded fabric, no adjustment is required. For asymmetrical patches all the same, left handers need to reverse again to achieve the patch shown. This can be accomplished by turning the fabric face down to cut it.

COMPARISON OF METHODS

Some common methods of rotary cutting can be improved upon and some so-called "shortcuts" are in fact no more than detours. I have studied the efficiency and accuracy of various methods and shortcuts and have formed some definite opinions, which I discuss in this chapter.

CROSSWISE STRIP METHOD

Description. Crosswise strips are cut across the width of folded fabric. Each strip is 40"-44" long with the crosswise grain of the fabric along the long edge of the strip.

Advantages. Crosswise strips, being longer, sometimes result in a few more patches per yard. You can cut long patches from ⅛- and ¼-yard pieces.

Disadvantages. The crosswise grain is stretchier and less stable than the lengthwise grain. The print often veers seriously off the crosswise grain. Furthermore, the fabric's fold may not be perpendicular to the crosswise threads.

I don't recommend cutting crosswise strips through more than two layers. Folds don't stack neatly enough to permit four layers that won't shift, and accuracy will suffer. Sometimes you must unfold the fabric for asymmetrical patches or to get an extra patch at the fold. Care must be taken to cut crosswise strips at perfect right angles to the fold in order to assure a straight strip instead of one that jogs.

Recommendations. Crosswise strips are the norm in rotary cutting, in spite of the fact that lengthwise strips offer distinct advantages. I would strongly recommend that novices rotary cut lengthwise strips exclusively. I would also recommend that quilters who learned rotary cutting using crosswise strips consider changing to lengthwise for some, if not all, applications. The measurements and cutting procedures don't change at all from crosswise to lengthwise. It is a simple matter of the strip being parallel to one grain instead of the other. However, I understand the resistance to change, so my charts include crosswise information as well as lengthwise.

A BETTER METHOD: LENGTHWISE STRIPS

Description. Lengthwise strips are cut parallel to the selvedge, usually through four layers of stacked fabric. The procedure is not very different from crosswise strips. Lengthwise strips can be made using the same strip and patch dimensions used for crosswise strips. You simply make the first cut parallel to the selvedge. If you like, you can convert a pattern designed for crosswise strips to lengthwise. The number of strips will stay about the same if you use ⅝-yard lengths, with each two layers equalling one 44" strip.

Advantages. The lengthwise grain is more stable and less stretchy than the crosswise grain. On any fabric, the printed pattern aligns perfectly with the lengthwise grain, but often does not follow the crosswise thread. Because there is no fold, the fabrics lay perfectly flat and are easier to align and cut precisely.

With shorter strips, you will need 2½ times as many 18" strips to yield the same number of patches as crosswise strips. This means more fabric variety for scrap quilts. You don't have to maneuver an unwieldy 24" ruler; 19" will do nicely.

With lengthwise strips, your strip length is not constrained by the fabric width. You can customize strip length according to the patch dimensions in order to minimize fabric waste. For example, you can cut 9½" squares from a 19" long strip with no waste. If you cut them from a 41" to 44" crosswise strip, you would have 3" to 6" of waste.

Lengthwise strips can be used for strip piecing, where they are short enough to hold in the proper alignment as you feed them into the sewing machine.

Even though many shapes for rotary cutting end up with sides on both the lengthwise grain and the crosswise grain, you will do better to start with a lengthwise cut. It's always best to start with your best foot forward. For some shapes, such as diamonds, two sides are on the straight grain and two on the bias. Lengthwise strips yield a lengthwise edge and a bias edge, whereas crosswise strips yield a less stable crosswise edge and a bias one.

Disadvantages. The yardage may be slightly greater for 18" lengthwise strips. However, you can customize strip length for less fabric waste than you get with crosswise strips. For lengthwise strips you will need to cut off a length of fabric before cutting strips if you are using long yardage.

Recommendations. Experienced seamstresses and quiltmakers know that the lengthwise grain of the fabric is more stable than the crosswise grain. (Recall that dressmaking patterns have you align grain arrows parallel to the selvedges.)

You can see for yourself how much better the lengthwise grain is by doing two simple tests. Hold a piece of fabric with your hands 6" or 8" apart on the crosswise grain. Bring your hands together, then quickly pull the fabric outward with a snap. Now, repeat on the lengthwise grain. Even with the selvedge removed, the lengthwise grain is significantly firmer, as you will note by the crisp snap on the lengthwise grain as opposed to the dull thud on the crosswise. Now hold the fabric with your hands shoulder width apart, and stretch gently, first on the crosswise grain, then on the lengthwise grain. Note how much more it stretches on the crosswise grain.

Why on earth would anyone want to cut crosswise strips when lengthwise strips are clearly better? It is easy to switch to cutting 18" lengthwise strips from half yards and fat quarters. Give lengthwise strips a try. Let the perfect grain instantly improve your patchwork.

STRIP PIECING

Description. Strip piecing is useful for making rows of squares, rectangles, diamonds, or parallelograms from strips instead of individual shapes. In this method, you start by cutting strips and sewing them together into "strip sets." Then you subcut the strip sets. For angled cuts, you must stagger the strips as you join them.

Lone Star, Trip Around the World and Irish Chain quilts are well suited to this method. For many other quilts and blocks, strip piecing can be used to make some of the units. For example, the 9-Patch and striped units in a Young Man's Fancy block can be readily strip pieced and later combined with conventionally-pieced triangle units and plain squares.

Strip piecing uses the same patch dimensions required for patch cutting. The difference is that in strip piecing, strips are cut, then *sewn before subcutting.* The cutting angles and subcutting dimensions are the same for strip piecing as for rotary patches. You can use the charts in this book regardless of whether you subcut before or after stitching.

Advantages. Strip piecing is unquestionably efficient. Strips can be cut through four layers. This method also minimizes the number of seam allowances you need to press.

Disadvantages. Subcuts made after stitching should be done through one layer only. It is hard to cut accurately through bumpy seamed strip sets. You can't backtack every seam when you strip piece. Some quiltmakers' acccuracy suffers when they strip piece. This method can be tricky to visualize and convoluted to describe. It seriously limits the variety of fabric combinations in scrap quilts. Finally, strip piecing possibilities are somewhat limited in traditional-style patchwork.

Recommendations. While I cannot complain about the efficiency of strip piecing, it is a method I prefer not to use. I like to backtack each seam to reinforce it. Furthermore, I want to make any pattern that inspires me. Many block and quilt designs cannot be accomplished with strip piecing shortcuts.

Nonetheless, many quilters love the method and use strip piecing wherever possible.

SHORTCUTS & DETOURS

In order to distinguish the shortcuts from the detours, I studied the relative efficiencies of the methods that follow. I counted seams to be sewn and cutting strokes needed for units made from rotary cut patches in stacks of four. I compared these totals to the number of seams and cutting strokes for making the same number of units using various shortcuts. I think the results will surprise you.

ROTARY CUTTING PATCHES

Description. To rotary cut patches, cut a single stack of strips first. Leave the strip stack in place on the mat, and pull the remaining fabric an inch or so away from the strip. When you rotary cut the strip stack, you can also cut along one end of the ruler to clean up the raw edge for subcutting squares or rectangles. Right handers clean up the bottom or left end. Left handers clean up the bottom or right end. For diamonds, hexagons, trapezoids, or triangle strips, clean up the end separately, at the angle indicated for your shape.

Usually, subcuts are parallel to this squared or angled end cut. These cuts are frequently made using the same ruler you used to cut the strip. Occasionally, the directions call for a different ruler. Often, you can use a shorter ruler to make subcuts efficiently. Position your rotary ruler to measure the listed distance from the end cut. Make parallel subcuts. If you will be making further subcuts, gently slide the strip between cuts to allow space between units.

Sometimes, subcuts are not parallel to the end, but measurements are still made relative to the end cut. See instructions for the individual patch shapes.

Continue with the subsequent cuts described for your shape. These cuts may involve cutting the unit in half diagonally or cutting off one or more corners, for example. These steps may require a special ruler. When you subcut strips into squares or other shapes, keep handling to a minimum. Leave the strip in place and turn the ruler and/or mat as needed. Complete the patch cutting before going on to the next strip.

While the patches are still in neat stacks of four, trim any 45° points using Judy Martin's Ultimate Point Trimmer. After the patches are completely cut and trimmed, set them aside and proceed with additional strips and patches from the same fabrics. When you have cut all strips and patches from one stack of fabrics, go on to another stack of fabrics.

Advantages. The rotary cut patches method is the most versatile. Contrary to popular belief, rotary cutting patches is often faster than so-called "short-cuts." Sewing is accomplished very quickly and effortlessly when you don't have to interrupt it to make additional cuts. Rotary cutting patches allows for total freedom in scrap fabric placement. It lets you reinforce each seam with backtacking, which can cut down on the aggravation of restitching unravelled seams. With rotary cut patches, the piecing is more straightforward. It is easy to visualize how the desired units result from the sewing steps. You can also cut through four layers every step of the way, with no seams to distort your cutting.

Disadvantages. Rotary cutting patches results in more pieces to feed into the sewing machine. You will have some bias edges, so you will want to learn how to master them. All of the cutting precedes the sewing, so it takes awhile to see results. If you are impatient for results or want to test the pattern, you may want to cut some of the patches and sew them before cutting more.

Efficiency. I tested various methods for making square units comprising half-square triangles. The efficiency rating for rotary cut half-square or pre-trimmed triangles as described on pages 34–37 is 100%. This is the best possible rating. It is the benchmark for triangle units. The pretrimmed method on pages 36–37 has the further advantage of yielding 16 more units per yard than any other method.

If you want units with all points trimmed, as I recommend, you will need to trim the remaining point of the triangles on pages 36–37. With trimming, this remains the top-rated method at 100% efficiency. Cutting half-square triangles as shown on pages 34–35 and then trimming points is 81% as efficient.

Recommendations. I find that rotary cutting patches is more efficient than all of the shortcuts except strip piecing. It is also versatile and accurate. Cutting out shapes gets a bad rap simply because it seems closer to traditional methods. When strip piecing won't do the job (or if you don't care for it), look to rotary cut patches for time savings, design freedom, and straightforward methods.

TRIANGLE GRIDS
Description. The triangle grids technique is a way of making square units having two contrasting half-square triangles sewn together on the long side. Instead of cutting individual triangles, in this method you cut two large rectangles of fabric arranged face to face. You mark one with a grid, and you sew on the grid lines before cutting into completed square units. The marking can be done with a pencil and ruler or with an iron-on transfer. To avoid marking, you can sew with a printed paper grid over the fabric.

Advantages. With this method, you will have fewer patches to feed into the sewing machine. You won't have to handle small patches, you can get started sewing right away, and you can avoid bias edges.

Disadvantages. With triangle grids, you will need to pin the fabrics together. Seams are longer. You need to handle a big piece. You must buy foundations or transfer sheets or measure and mark the grids yourself. You can subcut units through two layers only. You can't backtack each seam for durability. You must rip out a few stitches at the corners of units. You won't be able to have much scrap variety. Markings may show through if you are not careful. For the paper method, you must use a shorter stitch length, which can be difficult to rip out, and you must pick out paper shreds after sewing.

Efficiency. The efficiency rating for triangle grids using the iron-on method is 100%. It is 91% as efficient to measure and mark triangle grids. Efficiency is 86% for paper grids. These numbers are not far behind rotary cut patches, but they do not represent a shortcut.

When you trim the points, as I recommend, the efficiency drops seriously for triangle grid methods. Efficiency for iron-on grid units drops to 58%. Efficiency becomes 56% for the measure-and-mark method. Efficiency falls to 54% for paper grid methods. Trimmed grid triangles are nearly twice the work of trimmed rotary cut patches.

Recommendations. In my opinion, triangle grids are overrated. Simply rotary cutting patches is as efficient as the iron-on method and more efficient than paper grids or measure-and-mark grids. If you want to trim the points, grid methods are far less efficient than rotary cut triangles. They have other drawbacks, as well. The triangle grids method looks more like a detour than a shortcut to me.

TRIANGLE SQUARES
Description. Triangle squares is another way of making square units having two half-square triangles sewn together on the long side. Here, you cut two sets of two strips face to face. Then you cut these paired strips into small light and dark squares. You sew two seams ¼" on either side of the diagonal in each pair of squares, and cut in half diagonally between stitching lines to complete two units.

Advantages. With the triangle squares method you can avoid bias edges without having to mark a grid, handle a big piece, rip out stitches, or pick out paper shreds. You can backtack at the ends of each seam, and you can have good scrap variety.

Disadvantages. The final cut will be through two layers only. If you desire to trim points, you will have to do it through two layers only. You will have to mark cutting and/or sewing lines or use a special seam gauge to stitch ¼" from the diagonal .

Efficiency. The efficiency rating for triangle squares is 86%, a little worse than rotary cut patches.

Efficiency of the triangle squares method falls to 54% with points trimmed, nearly twice the work of rotary cut and pretrimmed units.

Recommendations. Triangle squares are more a detour than a shortcut. They have fewer disadvantages than the grid methods. If you are seriously challenged by bias edges, you might want to try the triangle squares method. Otherwise, stick with regular rotary-cut shapes.

PAPER PIECING

Description. Paper piecing involves the use of a printed paper pattern as a foundation. Roughly cut patches are positioned on the back of the paper; then the paper is turned over and stitched along the printed sewing lines. After seaming, excess is trimmed from the seam allowances, and the patch is pressed over the seam into its proper place. Other patches are added one at a time to cover the entire paper foundation. When the sewing is complete, the paper is torn away from the block or unit.

Advantages. Paper Piecing is useful for making blocks with exotic shapes and sharp, stretchy points. The results are generally precise. The sewing lines are easy to follow. People with questionable cutting and sewing skills can get pretty good results this way.

Disadvantages. Paper piecing is fussy. Before sewing on the line, you must align each patch in its sewing position on the back of the paper. If you roughly cut the patch extra large, you waste fabric. If you don't, you'll have to check both the front and back of the paper to see if the patch covers its space properly.

The paper piecing method is time-consuming. You must cut an approximate patch and then trim it again after sewing. This trimming is through one layer only, using scissors. You must take tiny stitches, which are hard to rip out if you make a mistake. You must tear away the paper when the unit is done. You cannot align the grain very precisely, you waste some fabric, and you use a lot of paper needlessly. The paper piecing method works for some, but not all, sewing situations.

Efficiency. Paper piecing has an efficiency rate of 50%. That is, it is twice the work of rotary cut patches. You could improve the efficiency of this method by cutting the patch the right size in the first place, eliminating the need to trim it later. However,

it might be difficult to position it accurately on the paper foundation. Come to think of it, if you cut it accurately, you wouldn't need a paper foundation, would you?

Recommendations. Paper piecing is definitely not a shortcut. I think paper piecing was developed as a way to cut and sew unusual shapes without traditional templates. Now there are better ways. Many shapes previously considered not suitable for rotary cutting are shown in this book. In my opinion, rotary cut patches paired with good sewing skills yield even better results than paper piecing.

Paper piecing is not for me. That is not to say there isn't a place for it. For beginners or people who have trouble sewing an even ¼" seam, paper piecing may be a means to reasonable results.

STITCH & FLIP

Description. With this method, squares and rectangles are cut and sewn to make Snowballs, Bow Ties, trapezoids, parallelograms, triangles, prisms, and such. For example, to make a Snowball block comprising an uneven octagon with four triangles in the corners, you start by cutting one large square and four small squares. Then you sew a small square to each corner of the large square, stitching diagonally from corner to corner of the small square.

Advantages. With this method you can avoid bias edges and cut easy, familiar shapes to make more exotic ones. Points don't need to be trimmed.

Disadvantages. The method requires a marked sewing line, guesswork, or a special seam gauge. You really should trim away the extra layers after stitching, which is fussy and takes twice as much time as cutting the shapes through four layers in the first place. If you don't trim away the extra layers, quilting will be difficult and show-through almost inevitable.

Efficiency. The stitch and flip method requires more yardage than the rotary cutting method on pages 36–37. It added 1⅝ yards (42%) in my test example. This method also wastes time. Even though you don't have to trim points with this method, it is only 81% as efficient as rotary cutting patches with all points trimmed.

Recommendations. In my opinion, the stitch and flip method is not a shortcut; it is just a bad idea. I don't understand the popularity of this method. Easy directions are provided in this book for more efficient ways to cut and sew the same blocks and units you get from stitching and flipping. Try simply rotary cutting the shapes you need. See how much time and fabric you will save. Then, please, go out and spread the word.

ROTARY CUTTING TECHNIQUES

A handful of techniques come up over and over again in rotary cutting. Some of these are quite familiar. Others are brand new. Don't try using the charts and directions until you are familiar with the following techniques.

CUT STRIP WIDTHS

Strips may be cut either lengthwise or crosswise. Furthermore, you can arrange the fabrics and cut the strips with strokes from side to side or away from your body. The cutting dimensions remain unchanged, and the charts provide yield information for both methods.

Cut Lengthwise Strips (Short Strips)

These are the preferred strips, with the long side of the strip parallel to the lengthwise grain. They are generally 18" long, cut from fat quarters or half yard lengths. If desired, you can adjust the length to use quarter yards or cut any length up to your ruler length. This lets you adjust for patch sizes or fabric on hand.

Because quilters are accustomed to placing the fabric with the selvedges parallel to the front edge of the cutting table, I suggest that you arrange Short Strips that way, too. However, you lay your ruler with its long sides parallel to the front edge of the table, and cut from right to left or left to right.

Short Strips from Fat Quarters or Half Yards. Short strips can be readily cut from fat quarters or half-yard lengths of fabric. For a quilt with a scrap look, stack four different unfolded fabrics to make four layers. Align and press enough of each fabric to cut the needed strips.

Different fabrics may vary in length; align their selvedges and align their raw ends on the left end for right handers or the right end for left handers.

Place the selvedges a few inches from the front of the table. (This space is to support the width of your ruler as you trim the selvedge.) Lay the ⅜" ruling (or whatever is needed) on the selvedge. Using a side-to-side stroke, cut through all layers along the edge of the ruler that is away from your body. This makes a clean-cut edge.

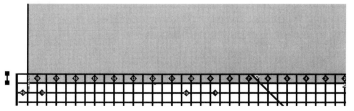

To cut the strip, slide the ruler up from the clean cut to the desired strip width. Align the appropriate ruling with the clean edge of the fabric and cut along the ruler's edge, parallel to the ruling.

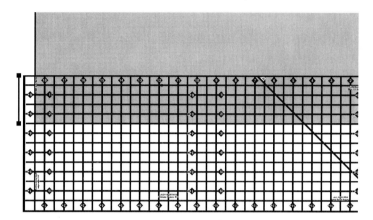

At this time, you can also cut along one short end of the ruler to clean up the raw edge if you will be subcutting squares or rectangles.

When you subcut strips into squares or other shapes, leave the strip in place and turn the ruler as needed. Plan to cut a strip, subcut it into patches, and trim the points of the patches before cutting the next strip.

Warning: Note that if you need mirror images from unfolded fabric, you must alternate face up and face down fabrics or subcut every two strips as reverses of each other.

Short Strips from Long Yardage. If you will be cutting many strips from the same fabric, you may cut the fabric into 18" lengths (or any other length up to 24" if you prefer). You can stack the pieces for up to four layers and cut as described above. This avoids folds and keeps your stacks of fabric flat and even.

If you don't mind a fold, or if your yardage is sufficiently long that you won't need to be cutting near the fold, you can fold and press the fabric in half lengthwise, selvedge to selvedge, then fold and press in half crosswise, aligning the two raw edges in one direction and all four selvedges in the other. I usually press up to, but not over, the folds. Trim the selvedge, cut off an 18" length now (or you can do it strip by strip) and begin cutting 18" strips from the selvedge toward the bolt's lengthwise fold. If you still need more strips, start over again, cutting additional 18" strips from the remaining fabric.

Warning: Note that if you fold the fabric you will get mirror images of asymmetrical shapes when you subcut. If you do not need mirror images, stack unfolded fabrics all facing the same direction.

Cut Crosswise Strips

Most quilters have learned to cut strips crosswise. I personally never use crosswise strips. You will need to make a clean cut before you cut the first strip. If you don't have two rulers as described below, you may need to turn the fabric, rotate the mat, or go to the opposite side of the table to do this.

Here's one way to cut crosswise strips. Fold the fabric in half lengthwise with right sides out and selvedges together. Place the fabric on the cutting mat with the fold an inch or two from the front edge of the mat. Lay a long, wide ruler or a big, square ruler over the fabric close to the left end (right handers) or the right end (left handers). The ruler's cutting edge should be close to the skimpiest part of the fabric end. Align a crosswise ruling with the fold. Place a second long ruler next to the first, covering the end of the fabric. Remove the first ruler. Cut along the long edge of the ruler. Start at the fold and head away from your body, trimming off a sliver to make a clean edge at right angles to the fold.

In order to cut the first strip, measure, laying the appropriate rule line (identified in the charts here as the cut strip width) on the clean edge at the end of the fabric. Cut parallel to the rule line along the edge of the ruler, starting at the fold and continuing away from your body.

To make sure your strips remain at right angles to the fold, align a crosswise ruling with the fold when you align the lengthwise ruling with the clean-cut edge.

As with lengthwise strips, plan to cut a strip, subcut it into patches, and trim the points of the patches before cutting the next strip.

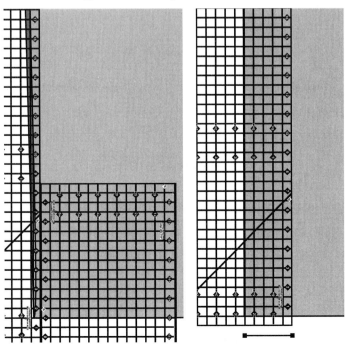

Warning: Note that if you fold the fabric you will get mirror images of asymmetrical shapes when you subcut. If you do not need mirror images, stack unfolded fabrics all facing the same direction. Also note that if you start subcutting at the selvedge end, you may be able to cut an extra patch at the fold.

CUT ANGLES

This is used for diamonds and parallelograms, among other shapes. The angles used are usually 45°, but occasionally 30° or 60°. You will find some or all of these angles on most rotary rulers. Start with a strip. Lay the appropriate angle line of your ruler even with one long edge of the strip. A triangular end of the strip will extend beyond the edge of the ruler. Cut off this triangle to match the cutting figures. The

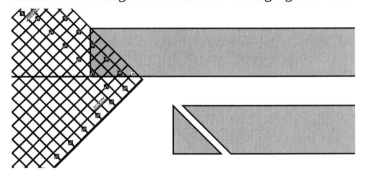

end of the strip is now angled perfectly for subcutting into patches. Usually, left handers cut off the lower right corner and right handers cut off the lower left corner of the strip.

PARALLEL SUBCUTS

This technique is used for cutting strips into squares, rectangles, diamonds, and more. Start with a strip. For squares and rectangles or other shapes to be cut from them, clean up one end of the strip at a right angle (perpendicular to the long edge of the strip). Lay the appropriate rule line on this right-angled end of the strip. Cut along the ruler's edge, parallel to the rule line and the end of the strip. The figures below show how to parallel subcut a square.

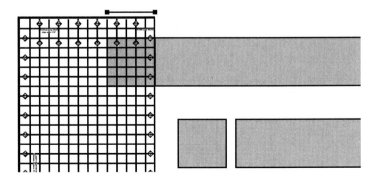

To parallel subcut a diamond, cut a strip and trim one end at the appropriate angle. Lay the desired

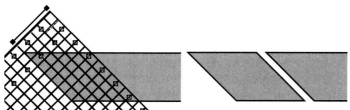

rule line over the angled end of the strip. Cut along the ruler's edge, parallel to the ruling to complete a diamond as shown above.

CUT IN HALF DIAGONALLY

This technique is used to make various triangles. Start with a square, rectangle, diamond, or parallelogram. Lay the edge of the ruler from one corner of the patch to its opposite corner. Cut the shape in half along the ruler's edge.

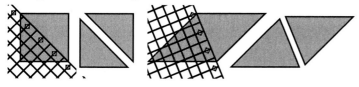

If two diagonal cuts are called for, keep the shapes together and perfectly aligned until you have completed both cuts.

TRIM A TRIANGLE

This technique is used for octagons, Snowballs, and Bow Ties, among other shapes. This is the most efficient method, although other methods are possible for some patch sizes. It requires the use of the Shapemaker 45 tool. Start with a square or rectangle. Align the base (long side) of the S45 even with the edge of the patch. The listed ruling should align with the patch corner.

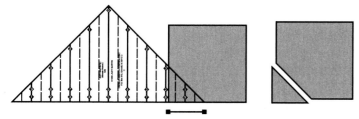

Cut along the angled end to trim off a triangle. Repeat as necessary to complete your shape.

TRIM 2 TRIANGLES

This is used for prisms, house shapes, and half prisms. It calls for a Shapemaker 45 tool. Start with a

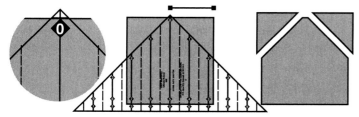

square or rectangle. Align the short line at the top of the S45 even with the edge of the patch. Center the midline (marked "0") of the S45 so that it is the listed distance from both sides of the patch. Cut along the two short sides of the S45 to trim off two triangles.

S45 SUBCUTS

This technique is used for triangle strips, trapezoids, and half trapezoids. It requires the use of the Shapemaker 45 tool. Start with a strip. Clean up the end of the strip at the appropriate angle. Using the S45, align the base of the tool even with the long edge of the strip.

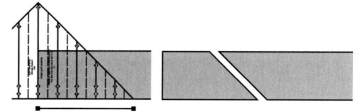

The appropriate ruling should align with the point or corner at the end of the strip. Cut along the angled short end of the tool to cut one shape off a strip. Rotate the tool to cut the next triangle or trapezoid from the strip. For half trapezoids, right angle subcut the next patch.

RIGHT ANGLE SUBCUTS

This technique is used for cutting half trapezoids from strips or 135° kites from triangles. For the half trapezoid, start with a a strip having a 45° angle at one end. Place your ruler's appropriate rule line at this pointed end, with the long edge of the strip or triangle even with any line that crosses the first ruling.

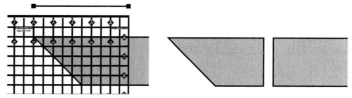

Cut along the edge of the ruler, parallel to the appropriate rule line. This cut is at a 90° angle to the long edge of the strip.

For 135° kites, start with a right triangle. Position the appropriate rule line at the point. Align any line

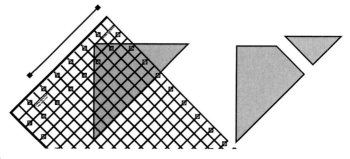

15

that crosses this ruling with the long edge of the triangle. Cut along the edge of the ruler at right angles to the long side of the triangle to complete a kite.

CUT 2:1 ANGLES

This technique lets you use a regular ruler to cut the triangles on page 49 or the kites on page 62. Choose a ruler, such as the R16, having a grid of squares one inch or smaller. On your ruler's grid, you will be counting two squares over to each one square down—or two squares down to one square over, whichever gives you the needed angle. For the triangle on page 49, lay the ruler over the long edge of the strip so that the fabric edge forms a line that diagonally crosses two-square rectangles, as shown.

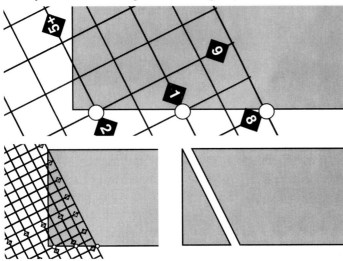

For the kite, position the corner of a grid square on the corner of the fabric square. Rotate the ruler until the square's edge makes a diagonal through 2:1 rectangles on the ruler's grid. Repeat on the other side of the same corner.

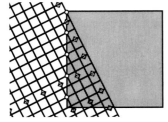 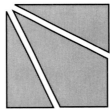

For either shape, rather than following a rule line or angle line, you follow the corners of 2:1 rectangles composed of two neighboring grid squares. You then cut along the edge of the ruler to trim off a triangle from the end of the strip or square at a 2:1 angle.

FOLD & TRIM

I came up with this trick as I worked on this book. It is a way to cut strip or patch dimensions that are hard to measure, but that, when doubled, can be easily managed. A perfect example is the shape known as "spike" or "recs," a half-rectangle triangle twice as long as it is wide. In order to cut the angle and dimensions correctly, the strip width for common sizes of this patch is in thirty-seconds of inches. If we double these sizes, we get sixteenths, which we can cut using the R16 or by going halfway between two eighths on a regular ruler. Doubling the strip width, then folding the strip in half, lets us cut two pieces exactly the size we need. I like to add ¼" to the doubled number because it is easier to trim off a fold than it is to cut along it.

Start the fold-and-trim technique by cutting the strip as listed. (The listed number is already double the size you would ordinarily cut it, plus ¼"). Crease the strip in half lengthwise, using an iron, to make it the cut width plus ⅛". Align the ⅛" line of your ruler even with the fold. Shave off ⅛" from each layer to make two separate strips of the desired width.

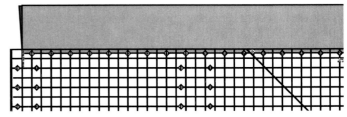

Proceed as usual to subcut the strips. Note that if the next cut yields asymmetrical patches, leave the strips or patches stacked as is for mirror images. If all patches must be the same, restack the strips or patches the same side up before subcutting.

CUT PARALLEL TO THE DIAGONAL

This technique is used for octagons, hexagons, diagonal prisms, and Snowballs. Start with a square, rectangle, or diamond. Lay the appropriate rule line diagonally from one corner to the opposite corner of the shape. Cut along the edge of the ruler, parallel to the diagonal. Repeat as needed to complete the shape. You may need to leave the cut parts in position for subsequent cuts.

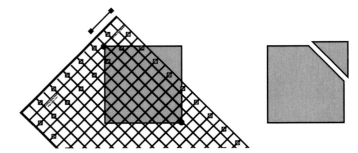

SPECIALTY TOOLS & THEIR USE

You may be interested in some rotary cutting tools beyond those discussed for the Deluxe Tool Kit. Here is a sampling of what is available. I'll start with the multipurpose tools and tools that can be put to good use frequently and move on to the more specialized ones.

The Rotaruler 16. This is a good, basic ruler, but if you already have a basic ruler, you may still want to consider the R16 as a specialty ruler. In addition to the standard rulings at ⅛" intervals, the R16 from Judy Martin's Ultimate Rotary Tools has complete rule lines for ¹⁄₁₆" intervals without the clutter of additional lines. This is accomplished by adding ¹⁄₁₆" to the outside edge on two adjacent sides of the ruler. Cutting along the clear edges gives you ordinary measurements. Cutting along the black edges yields ¹⁄₁₆ inches. You will need to pay attention to which edge you cut along when you use this ruler, but you will quickly learn to watch for the heavy black line.

Sixteenths can also be cut using an ordinary ruler simply by placing the fabric edge halfway between two eighths. However, if you prefer following an actual line, the R16 is the only ruler to offer this feature.

In the past, sixteenths didn't come up much. Sometimes, numbers were simply rounded to the nearest eighth (Unbelievable!), and sometimes designs were avoided since there was no accurate way to measure them. A glance through the charts, which list ¹⁄₁₆ inches the way the R16 does, with the next lower eighth followed by a "+," will demonstrate just how many useful patch shapes and sizes can be cut when you have a sixteenth ruler.

Omnigrid® 96 and 96L Triangles. These tools cut half-square triangles (having the short side on the straight grain). The rulings on these triangular tools are parallel to the two short sides. The #96 cuts triangles that finish up to 6" on the short side. The #96L cuts triangles that finish up to 8" on the short side. You can use either tool with the strip widths and yields from the chart on page 35, or you can use the tools with the chart on page 37 for triangles with one point pretrimmed. These tools use finished sizes and add the seam allowances automatically when you cut.

Start by using a regular ruler to cut a strip and to trim the end at a right angle. Lay the short edge of the triangle tool on the long edge of the strip. Align the appropriate numbered ruling with the trimmed end of the strip. Cut along the long edge of the tool. For the next triangle, lay the long edge of the tool on the angled cut from the last triangle. Align the appropriate ruling with the long side of the strip. For half-

square triangles using the chart on page 35, the point should touch the opposite long side of the strip. For pretrimmed triangles (page 37), the short yellow line nearest the point of the tool should be on the opposite long side. Cut along the short side of the tool. Repeat these two steps down the length of the strip.

Omnigrid® 98 and 98L Triangles. These tools cut quarter-square triangles from triangle strips, as shown on pages 40–41. The long sides of the triangles are on the straight grain. Either of the tools has rulings parallel to its long edge. Omnigrid® makes triangle tools in two sizes. The #98 cuts triangles that finish up to 8" on the long side; the #98L cuts them up to 12". The tools use finished dimensions and add seam allowances automatically.

Use the chart on page 40 for strip widths and yields. Cut the strip with a regular ruler. Cut off the end at a 45° angle. (You can use the triangle tool for this.) Lay the appropriate ruling on the long edge of the strip. (The black lines are for the whole inches numbered just above them.) Align one short side of the tool with the angled end of the strip. Cut along the other short side of the tool. Turn the tool to cut the next triangle.

Quilter's Rule™ Triangles QR-T6 or QR-T12. These tools cut quarter-square triangles from triangle strips as shown on pages 40–41. The big difference is that they cut triangles having the straight grain on the long side and nice dimensions on the short side. That is, the grain is opposite the usual grain. These tools come in handy for cutting edge triangles for diagonal sets. They are also useful for playing with stripes or for use in Virginia Reel blocks.

The tools comes in two sizes. The QR-T6 cuts triangles having finished short sides up to 6" long. The QR-T12 cuts triangles having finished short sides up to 12" long. Either tool lets you use finished dimensions and adds the seam allowances for you automatically. The finished sizes are shown with solid lines. For cutting, use the seam allowance lines, which are the dashed lines. The appropriate dashed cutting line is the one just below your desired finished size.

The chart on page 42 gives strip widths and yields for use with these tools. Cut the strip using a regular ruler. Then cut off the end of the strip at a 45° angle. (You can use the tool for this.) To cut a triangle, lay the dashed cutting line on the long edge of the strip. Position one short edge of the ruler on the angled end of the strip. Cut along the remaining short side of the ruler. Turn the ruler to cut the next triangle from the strip.

Rotary Mate Speedies. A speedy is a rotary cutting guide in the size and shape of a triangle that you want to cut off another shape. The Rotary Mate ruler from Patched Works, Inc. has the usual rulings as well as speedies in four sizes. Trudie Hughes has long used speedies to cut off triangles to turn a square or rectangle into a Snowball, Bow Tie, or other shape. She designed the Rotary Mate Ruler with speedies in 1", 1½", 2", and 2½" finished sizes. These numbers correspond to the finished short side of the triangle that you would sew onto the shape to make a square or rectangle again.

To use a speedy, lay the two short sides of the speedy on the corner of the fabric shape. Cut along the edge of the ruler to trim a triangle. The speedy automatically takes care of seam allowances.

My directions call for an S45 to trim a triangle. However, if you have a Rotary Mate but no S45, you can use a speedy instead to trim a triangle in four popular sizes. The charts list the size of triangle to trim using an S45. You will need to convert these sizes as follows for speedies: The 1" speedy corresponds to a 1⅛" trim; the 1½" speedy corresponds to a 1⅝" trim; the 2" speedy corresponds to a 2⅛" trim; and the 2½" speedy corresponds to a 2⅝" trim.

Master Piece® Static Stickers. These are translucent, colored acetate sheets backed with peel-off graph paper. They come in handy for rotary cutting odd shapes and sizes. Simply draw the desired patch on the graph paper backing, including seam allowances, and cut it out. If you prefer, peel off the backing, lay the acetate over a pattern, trace the cutting line, and cut. Stick the patch shape on the edge of your ruler. It holds in place by static electricity. Use the patch edges to guide you rather than using rule lines. For long strips, you can use a patch at each end of your ruler. You can reuse the Static Sticker patches, and you can turn them with different sides on the edge of the ruler for successive cuts.

These stickers were designed to go with the slotted Master Piece® rulers, but they work equally well with your regular ruler.

Add-A-Quarter™. This tool turns a traditional cardboard template in a finished size into a rotary cutting template. It is perfect for patches in odd sizes or shapes not found in this book.

Simply draft and cut out a cardboard or lightweight plastic template in the finished size of the patch. The tool has a lip ¼" wide along the long edge. Tape the template on the fabric with a minimum of ¼" of space all around. Align the lip of the tool, face down, with one edge of the template so that the ¼" lip extends beyond the template. Cut along the tool's edge through all layers of fabric. Keep the template in place, and similarly cut each side of the patch. This handy tool can help you rotary cut just about anything you can draft or trace.

Other Specialty Tools & Templates. A huge assortment of specialty tools and templates is available to help quilters rotary cut. Tools for one specific shape are generally self explanatory. They are usually limited to the most popular sizes. You may want to invest in a specialty tool if you expect to use the shape often or if you want the easiest possible way to cut a shape. Chart yields from this book should be similar to what you will get using a specialty tool, but the cutting dimensions and directions may vary from those in the book. Specialty tools you might want to consider are the 120° half-diamond and 60° equilateral triangle tools from Clearview Triangle; the Tri-Recs Tools™ set from EZ Quilting by Wrights®; and the Kaleido-Ruler from Marti Michell™.

Rotary templates are available in sets of compatible shapes and sizes or in sets for specific quilts. A template cuts a shape in one size only. Some templates are compatible with the strip widths and yields in this book. For others, you will be on your own.

It is usually more efficient to cut strips and patches as described in this book than it is to cut around a template. Sometimes, you can cut strips and then use templates for an efficient hybrid method. Templates are not really needed for a lot of shapes. However, some people prefer templates for their infallibility and straightforward simplicity. Templates are fine, but if you want to make a lot of different quilts, you can spend a fortune on the necessary templates. Multipurpose tools give you countless possibilities without the expense and clutter of templates.

I like multipurpose tools, and I limit the items in my toolbox accordingly. Some people prefer to have a tool for everything. I'll let you decide which specialty tools will enhance your quiltmaking.

ROTARY CUTTING QUESTIONS & ANSWERS

How Do I Cut Perfectly Accurate Patches?

Unlike old cutting methods, which tend to add a thread or two to the planned dimensions, rotary cutting is precise. This very precision can cause rotary cut quilts to come out skimpy. Every seam takes up a little of the patch size in going over the bulk of seam allowances. This take-up explains why everything works out according to plan in traditional template-and-scissor methods. Rotary cutting's more precise patches may not allow any extra for takeup. You may find your quilts turn out slightly smaller than anticipated when you rotary cut.

Perfectionists may want to compensate for take-up by adding a thread when cutting or by making seam allowances shallower by a thread. I prefer to adjust the cutting rather than the sewing. My reasoning is this: Rotary cutting dimensions for *some* shapes and sizes already include a little extra, just to make a nice number. Cutting dimensions for *other* patches are more precise and could use a little extra for take-up. The sewing can't be adjusted to deal with both kinds of patches, but cutting can be easily adjusted for each patch as needed.

In general, take-up is already included in measurements for cutting quarter-square, half-square, or any other isosceles right triangles. Align the rule line precisely over the clean-cut edge of the fabric. For any application of the Shapemaker 45 tool, center the short line at the top of the tool or align the base (long side) of the tool precisely on the fabric's edge.

In order to rotary cut squares, rectangles and most other shapes perfectly, you may want to adjust for take-up by adding a thread. To do this, lay the rule line one thread inside the clean edge of the fabric. For further details on whether or not to add a thread, see the paragraph about testing the pattern on page 8.

How Can I Prevent Ruler Slippage?

There are four secrets to prevent your ruler from slipping as you rotary cut along its edge.

1. Walk your hand down the ruler as you cut. By holding the ruler near where you are applying pressure with the rotary cutter, you can practically eliminate slippage altogether. Simply hold the cutter still as you adjust your grip on the ruler, then resume cutting.

2. Cut through four layers of fabric. The extra fabric thickness cushions the ruler and helps to keep it in place.

3. If you are still having trouble with slipping, you might benefit from self-adhesive sandpaper dots. Just

stick a few of these on the underside of the ruler to grip the fabric and hold the ruler in place.

4. Use a ruler that grips the fabric. The Quilter's Rule™ has raised lines on the bottom to keep the ruler in place on the fabric as you cut. I found this ruler extremely useful when I was a beginner.

How Can I Avoid Cockeyed-Looking Patches?

Patches look cockeyed when the print or the thread of the grain veers off at a slight angle to the cutting stroke. There are five simple solutions to this problem.

1. Cut lengthwise strips. The print and the thread follow the selvedge reliably. A long patch, such as a rectangle, looks its best when its long side follows the print and the thread of the lengthwise grain. If you cut strips on the crosswise grain, you will have to choose between the thread and the print, and neither of these may be at right angles to the fold.

2. Don't fold the fabric when you cut linear prints that you hope to align perfectly. You will want to see the pattern entirely and align your rulings with the printed or woven pattern for perfectly straight cuts.

3. You can still stack these linear fabrics. Simply put the plaids, stripes, and other linear patterns on the top of a stack of more forgiving prints whenever possible.

4. After laying your ruler over linear-patterned fabric, "tickle" your fabric into perfect alignment with the ruler. That is, use a light, scratching motion of your fingertips to work the fabric into position. Start with the fabric tucked under the ruler slightly too much, and with this gentle tickling motion, tease it out from under the ruler as much as is necessary.

5. Avoid prints that repeat in rows that veer off the sides of your patch. For example, if you have a dot pattern that is spaced a little differently in length and width, don't use it to cut a half-square triangle. The diagonal line of dots would veer off the true bias of the long side of the triangle. The same print might be perfectly all right for cutting squares, however.

How Can I Read My Ruler On Dark Fabric?

This is not as much a problem as you might think. You won't have any trouble seeing black rulings against a green, white, or gray mat. Your rulings will be perfectly clear if they contrast with either the mat or the fabric. Reading the numbers can be more difficult, but here are three easy solutions.

1. Flag the line you intend to follow before you lay it over your fabric. Small, self-adhesive dots are perfect for this. Simply stick a contrasting dot on the intended line on the face of the ruler. This makes measuring faster, since you only have to find the line once. It also helps prevent cutting mistakes. Flagging is useful even if your ruler contrasts well with your fabric. And stickers on the face of the ruler can be easily removed without harming the ink, which is on the underside of the ruler.

2. Use a ruler having numbering that contrasts with dark fabric. Trudie Hughes' rulers from Patched Works, Inc., printed with white numbers and rules, are perfect examples. Omnigrid's® yellow-and-black numbering also shows up well.

3. For scrap quilts or for quilts requiring the same patches from various shades, stack the lighter fabrics on top to make it easier to read black numbering.

How Can I Keep Fabric Stacks Even?

Cutting through four layers of fabric is a big time-saver for rotary cutting. However, if your fabrics shift, your accuracy will suffer. Here are four simple secrets to assure you of even stacks.

1. The biggest key to even stacks is pressing. Press each fabric, then press again as you stack each of the four layers together. The fabrics will stick to each other rather than shifting. It is not necessary to press the entire fabric if you are only cutting a few strips. However, press for a foot or so beyond the area you will be using in order to keep the working area flat and smooth.

2. For best results, use unfolded fabric or have the folds well beyond the working area. Of course, for crosswise strips you will be cutting each strip from the fold. This is one of the drawbacks of crosswise strips. One fold is tolerable, but two folded, stacked fabrics can mean trouble. Two folds won't stay neatly stacked. Creasing them well beyond the work area may help alleviate shifting, but you may not want a permanent crease in the center of your fabric.

3. After stacking fabrics, trim a sliver off the edge before you cut. Even if the fabrics already have a clean, straight edge with the selvedge removed, trimming the stack *together* will assure you of uniformly sized strips and patches for all layers.

4. Plan to minimize handling in your rotary cutting. Cut a strip and leave it where you cut it. Pull the fabric stack away from the strip to give you some room. Subcut the strip into patches right away, rather than putting it aside to subcut later. This way, the fabric stack never gets a chance to shift out of alignment. Before putting the patches aside, complete all subcutting and trim the points through all four layers. When the patches are completely cut and trimmed you can handle them as much as you want.

How Do I Cut Wide Strips and Big Patches?

A long ruler 6"–8" wide will serve to cut most patches. However, sometimes you need to cut something bigger, such as a 12½" alternate block. Here are some ideas for cutting the big strips and patches.

1. Get out your big square ruler and cut one or two patches at a time rather than cutting strips into patches. I especially like the 15" square Omnigrid® ruler for the big stuff.

2. Use two rulers. This is especially good for wide strips. Use the full width of a long ruler and add on to this as necessary with a second ruler. Say you want to cut a 9½"-wide strip and you have a 6" x 24" ruler and a 4" x 24" ruler. You will need the full 6" of the bigger ruler and 3½" of the smaller ruler. Lay the 3½" ruling of the 4"-wide ruler on the clean-cut edge of the fabric. Lay the 6"-wide ruler alongside the 4" ruler. Cut along the edge of the 6" ruler.

This is easiest if both rulers are long. However, if one ruler is short, a 4" square, for example, you can start by positioning the small ruler, aligning the appropriate ruling with the middle of the clean edge of the fabric. Lay the bigger ruler next to the small one, and slip the small ruler out without disturbing the big one. Reposition the small ruler at one end of the strip. Adjust the end of the big ruler as necessary to touch the small ruler. Repeat at the opposite end. Once the big ruler is perfectly in position, hold it firmly and cut. Don't worry about the small ruler.

Warning. When using two rulers, take care to notice ruler widths. Some rulers are in widths other than full inches. There are 3½" wide rulers, for example, and the Rotaruler 16 is 7¹⁄₁₆" wide. You may find it easier to use these odd-width rulers for the add-on measurement, and let the fraction at one edge of the ruler extend beyond the edge of the fabric. Cut along the edge of the ruler having a width in full inches.

How Do I Cut Reversals and Mirror Images?

Most of the common patches, such as squares and rectangles, are symmetrical; that is, they look the same face up or face down. These can be cut right or left handed, with fabric folded in half or unfolded, with the same results. Some other patches, such as long triangles and half trapezoids are asymmetrical. Special care must be taken to cut these according to your quilt plan. Here are some helpful guidelines.

1. Some quilts call for asymmetrical patches and their reverses in equal quantities. These mirror images are most readily cut from fabric folded in half.

2. Mirror images can also be cut from stacked fabrics, half of them face up and half face down.

3. Sometimes all asymmetrical patches in a quilt are alike. In such a case, you must *not* fold the fabric.

Furthermore, care must be taken to keep stacked fabrics all facing the same side up.

4. If your quilt calls for asymmetrical patches that are the reverse of the ones shown in the book, turn the fabric face down and cut as shown to achieve the desired results.

5. If you are cutting left handed, starting at the right end of the strip, you will get the reverse of the asymmetrical patches shown in this book. When cutting left handed, turn the fabric face down if you want to match the asymmetrical patch shown in the book.

How Do I Avoid Stretching the Bias?

The bias can stretch, but this is no reason to be intimidated. A few basic precautions will have you handling the bias like a pro. Quilters have devised countless detours to avoid bias edges. What they may not realize is that bias doesn't need to be cut in order to stretch. Improper handling can stretch bias whether the edge is cut or not. For perfect results, follow these simple guidelines.

1. Plan patch cutting so the straight grain of the fabric falls around the edges of blocks and units. Once all of the bias edges are stitched down, you can safely press the unit.

My one exception is for extra-long prisms, half prisms, trapezoids, and half trapezoids. Sometimes, I prefer to cut these with the long sides on the straight grain and the short ends on the bias, even when this puts the bias on the block's edges. Here, you should avoid ironing until the bias is stitched to the sash, border, or other segment.

2. As you rotary cut along the bias, hold the ruler extra firmly near the points of the patch. Don't let the fabric be pulled out from under the ruler at the point, or you may end up with some distortion. Of course, be sure to keep your fingertips out of the path of the rotary cutter.

3. As you feed patches into the sewing machine, hold them flat against the sewing machine bed. If the entire patch is flat, it cannot be stretched. Don't hold the fabric between your thumb and index finger after it reaches the machine bed. Instead, simply let your hands float over the fabric, keeping it flat at the seam line and clear off to the side of the seam. Don't push or pull the fabric, just guide it gently.

4. Pin long seams at regular intervals. Keep the work supported on a flat surface, such as a table or bed, as you pin.

5. Fingerpress units, rather than pressing or ironing, until the bias edges have been stitched. Then use a dry iron instead of steam and press (without moving the iron back and forth) or iron with the iron moving back and forth in the direction of the straight grain.

How Do I Rotary Cut a Scrap Quilt?

Rotary cutting is not just for quilts from a few fabrics. True scraps can be rotary cut, and scrap looks from yardage or fat quarters are also possible using the same techniques you use for other quilts. Just follow the directions, making these adjustments.

1. For a scrap look, use fat quarters or half yards and cut just one or two lengthwise strips from each fabric. Stack four different, unfolded fabrics, all face up. Short Strips (lengthwise) offer more scrap variety because you won't need to cut so many patches from a strip, and therefore, you won't get so many alike.

2. You can further enhance the scrap variety by cutting just one strip for several shapes from one fabric. Cut the widest strip needed, subcut a patch or two from it, then cut the remainder of the strip down to the next smaller strip width. Subcut another patch or two, and so on.

3. Avoid grid triangles and other such shortcuts. Rotary cutting patches will let you mix and match patches in limitless combinations for greatly improved scrap variety.

4. In order to cut patches from true scraps, first press each scrap and make a clean cut along the lengthwise grain. (You can follow a thread or the print to make this cut.) Stack as many as four different scraps, aligning their left ends (right handers) or their right ends (left handers), pressing as you add each piece. Trim a sliver off the clean edges with the fabrics stacked. Cut strips and patches as shown, stopping when the patches run off the end of the scraps. The listed yields will not apply, but you won't need to worry about yardage for a true scrap quilt.

WHAT PATCH DO I NEED?

IDENTIFYING THE SHAPE

Most of the patches in this book can be distinguished from one another at a glance. The drawings in the book are scale drawings showing actual angles and proportions.

Many shapes, such as rectangles, trapezoids, and prisms, are available in several proportions, as indicated in parentheses in the chart title and described in the paragraph introducing the shape. A graph grid or patch measurements should help you identify proportions to match the chart and figures.

Triangles are sometimes identified by proportions, but more often by angles. Some triangles look somewhat similar to each other. Distinguish them by angles or patch families.

Patch Families. Usually, triangles and other shapes are used in families with compatible angles. Patch families are mentioned in the description paragraphs for a shape. Below are some block examples showing common patch families.

CHOOSING A PATCH SIZE

You can choose the patch size first and build up to a block size, or you can start with a block size and divide into grid units to determine patch sizes. For some blocks having true diamonds, octagons, or tilted squares or rectangles, you will want to start with a Magic Measure (see the next section).

Finished dimensions of all sides of a patch are listed in the chart for each shape. These will help you figure dimensions of neighboring patches. It is really very easy. Pick a size for one patch. Find that patch in your block drawing. See what else has that dimension. Perhaps the block is divided into grid units of that size. Perhaps the grid is half that size or twice

that size. Even if there is no grid, you can determine the sizes of other patches by their relationships to the first patch and each other. Neighboring patches often have matching sides. If so, they are the same dimension on that side. The chart for each shape will tell you the dimensions of the other sides of the patch to help you size the patches that touch them. Sometimes the finished dimension listed in the chart has been rounded to the nearest 1/16", but you can still use these figures to match sizes.

Here are some basic rules to get you started:

1. Think of *finished* sizes, not cut sizes to determine patch relationships in a block.

2. When two patches share a side for their whole length, that side is the same size in both patches. That is,

same side = same size.

3. When two or more patches joined together extend from one end to the other of a single patch, the big patch side equals the sum of the small patch sides.

On the facing page is a chart listing block and unit sizes for grid blocks and octagon- or LeMoyne Star-based blocks. Simply find the row for your desired unit size, and follow it to the right to the column for your grid or octagon. Where row and column meet, you will find your block size.

MAGIC MEASURES

Magic Measures are special sizes for rotary cutting. They make it easy to rotary cut patches that would be difficult to measure in other sizes.

When some patches, such as squares and rectangles, are tilted in the block, the measuring can get

2:1 Angle Family
This block uses several related shapes from pages 26, 48, 49, & 62.

Octagon Family
This block uses related shapes from pages 26, 40, 50, 51, 56, & 63.

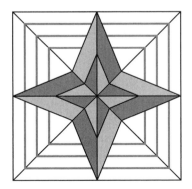

22½° Angle Family
This block uses related shapes from pages 43, 44, & 71.

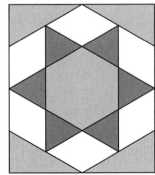

Hexagon Family
This block uses the shapes on pages 46, 47, 54, & 55.

Block Sizes for Various Unit Sizes & Grid or Octagon Sizes

Unit Size	Grid 2 x 2	Grid 3 x 3	Grid 4 x 4	Grid 5 x 5	Grid 6 x 6	Grid 7 x 7	Grid 8 x 8	Octagon
⅞"	1¾"	2⅝"	3½"	4⅜"	5¼"	6⅛"	7"	3"
1"	2"	3"	4"	5"	6"	7"	8"	—
1+	2⅛"	3⅛+	4¼"	5¼+	6⅜"	7⅜+	8½"	3⅝"
1¼"	2½"	3¾"	5"	6¼"	7½"	8¾"	10"	4¼"
1½"	3"	4½"	6"	7½"	9"	10½"	12"	5⅛"
1¾"	3½"	5¼"	7"	8¾"	10½"	12¼"	14"	6"
2"	4"	6"	8"	10"	12"	14"	16"	—
2⅛"	4¼"	6⅜"	8½"	10⅝"	12¾"	14⅞"	17"	7¼"
2½"	5"	7½"	10"	12½"	15"	17½"	20"	8½"
3"	6"	9"	12"	15"	18"	—	—	10¼"
3⅛+	6⅜"	9½+	12¾"	15⅞+	19⅛"	—	—	10⅞"
3½"	7"	10½"	14"	17½"	—	—	—	12"
3⅝"	7¼"	10⅞"	14½"	18⅛"	—	—	—	12⅜"
4"	8"	12"	16"	20"	—	—	—	—

tricky using other sizes. Likewise, for non-grid blocks based on octagons or true 45° diamonds, the measuring can be a problem. With Magic Measures, each finished side of a patch, as well as the block size, can be readily measured and rotary cut.

I discovered the first few Magic Measures quite by accident. When I saw how they could help my rotary cutting, I did some math (Don't try this at home!) to find more of these handy numbers.

Magic Measures may not be the first numbers that you think of for patch sizes. (I'd guess most people think of 2" first.) However, they come in very handy, and you should definitely keep them in mind.

For those tricky situations, simply substitute 2⅛" patches for 2" ones, adjust the other patch sizes correspondingly, and rotary cut with ease. I include Magic Measures in all of my cutting charts, and I use them for at least half of my patterns now. Remember Magic Measures when you want to simplify your rotary cutting. Some of your favorite sizes happen to be Magic Measures. Here are the two main families of Magic Measures:

¾", 1+, 1½", 2⅛", 3", 4¼", 6", 8½", 12"
and
⅝", ⅞", 1¼", 1¾", 2½", 3½"

Now you can see where I got some of the patch sizes listed in my charts! Believe me, these are not weird numbers at all compared to the ones you would need without Magic Measures!

The relationships of Magic Measures within a family are best illustrated in the graphics below. Study these figures if you want to understand why Magic Measures work. Of course, you don't need to *understand* Magic Measures to use them any more than you need to understand electricity to turn on a light. Simply using Magic Measures when you rotary cut will give you all their advantages.

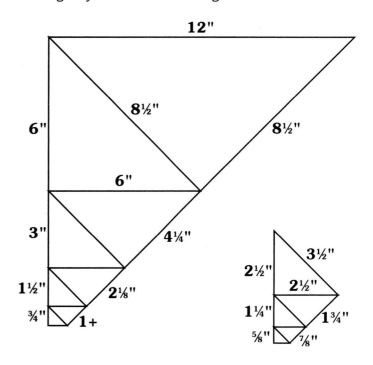

Magic Measures

USE OF THE CUTTING CHARTS

Don't let charts intimidate you. A chart is simply a group of lists. On each chart on the following pages you'll find a list of finished sizes, a list of cutting measurements, and a list of yields to help you with yardages. A single shape in a number of sizes is featured in each chart.

An index to the charts is on page 80. Additional charts for some shapes feature variations in proportions, grainlines, or methods.

Most shapes and sizes can be cut using just a regular ruler. Some of the bigger sizes must be cut using two rulers (page 20) or a big square ruler. When a tool other than a regular ruler or a big ruler is required, the headline above the chart indicates so.

Above each chart or on the facing page you will find step-by-step directions and illustrations showing how to cut the shape. As you grow accustomed to the techniques and terms used in this book, you should be able to cut shapes simply by glancing at the charts. At first, you may need to look over the illustrations, as well. For unfamiliar shapes and methods, you will appreciate the step-by-step directions.

HOW DO I USE THE CHARTS?

Each line in a chart tells finished dimensions, cutting dimensions, and yield for a single size patch. Step-by-step directions and illustrations are labeled with letters to correspond with the letters heading the columns in the charts. The description columns help you identify your desired size; the cutting columns tell you what size to cut your patch, with seam allowances included; and the yield columns help you with yardage. To use a chart, find the line for your particular finished size and follow it to the right to the columns for rotary cutting dimensions and yield.

The Description Columns. The dimension of each side of the patch is listed in a separate column at the left of the chart. Where it is helpful, the overall patch length or width is also listed. Each column is lettered, and patch illustrations are lettered to match. Note that the side listed in the description column is shown in the corresponding illustration by a solid line ending in two dots.

I tried to include the most useful patch sizes and shapes that can be rotary cut. The most common patch sizes are listed, as well as Magic Measures sizes (page 22), which are the best sizes for rotary cutting true octagons, diagonal squares, patches for true 8-pointed stars, and many shapes that would be difficult to measure accurately in other sizes.

Often, one side of a patch will be a nice, familiar number and another side will be not so nice. Usually, you identify the patch by the nice side. Listing *all* sides helps you identify neighboring patches. You simply need to remember that patches that share a side are the same size on that side. Dimensions in the description columns are rounded to the nearest sixteenth of an inch. You can match these dimensions to each other in order to identify the right patch sizes for your quilt, whether they are rounded or not.

The Cutting Columns. These columns in the middle of the chart tell you the rotary cutting dimensions for the patch in step-by-step sequence. Seam allowances of ¼" are already included in the listed numbers. Cutting dimensions are the same for lengthwise or crosswise strips. Note that each column is labeled with a letter to correspond with the lettered illustrations and step-by-step directions. The column heads are necessarily brief. Study the illustrations and step-by-step narrative for further details.

The Yield Columns. These columns at the right of each chart tell how many patches you can cut from a strip and how many patches you can cut from a yard of fabric. There are four columns, the first two for lengthwise strips 18" long, the second two for crosswise strips about 44" long. The yield per strip should be quite different for 18" and 44" strips. The yield per yard is similar, the difference mainly coming from the fact that the 18" strips are cut from two half yard pieces rather than a whole yard.

The yield figures allow for some variation in fabric width and minimal shrinkage. They do not allow for cutting errors. Depending on the actual usable length and width of your fabric, you may get a slightly higher or lower yield. You should always allow extra, just to be safe, when you buy fabric for a project.

The Cutting Directions. The chart lists the dimensions to be cut in each step, and the step-by-step instructions above the chart or on the facing page provide more details. There are eleven techniques used for the rotary cutting in this book. I have named each of these and used the name in the rotary cutting directions for each shape. You may be familiar with several of these techniques. Others are introduced in this book for the first time. If the directions refer you to a technique described elsewhere in the book, be sure to read the reference, at least the first time you encounter it. It may not be what you expect. You just might learn a new technique.

The Cutting Illustrations. These are to the right of the directions and show, at a glance, what space you are measuring with the listed numbers. My figures show lengthwise strips. Turn the figures sideways to visualize crosswise strips. The measured distance is shown in the figure with a solid line ending in two squares. The figures will probably be perfectly clear to you for the common shapes. For the more exotic shapes, you will quickly learn what the figures mean, but at first you may need to look at the step-by-step directions for explanation.

Efficiency. Sometimes, an intermediate shape is cut, and then it is trimmed or cut in half to make the desired shape. When the last intermediate shape runs off the end of the strip, you may still be able to use the partial shape. If you can get one useful patch from a partial shape, I assume you will do so. In the interests of efficiency, I have counted these patches in the yield charts.

Patch Families. Some patches look fairly similar to others having different angles or proportions. To help you distinguish these, in the introductory paragraphs for the shapes I have mentioned patches that are often used in combination with each other. An example would be the hexagon family, which also includes the 60° diamond, 30°-60°-90° triangle, and equilateral triangle.

WHAT DO "+" AND "(-)" MEAN?

Numbers Followed by "+." Basically, the "+" indicates that you need to add ¹⁄₁₆" to the listed measurement. I could have listed sixteenths, but quilters are more accustomed to working in eighths. The "+" notation is actually in a more useful form because in order to measure sixteenths you use the next lower eighth and add a sixteenth to it. On a regular ruler you do this by going halfway between the listed number and the next higher eighth. On the Rotaruler 16, the only ruler to have lines for measuring sixteenths, you follow the line labeled just like the chart notation, and the ruler automatically adds the sixteenth when you cut along the black edge.

The "+" notations may be in the description columns or the cutting columns. When they are in the description columns, you won't need to measure them, so don't worry about having a special ruler for these numbers.

Numbers Followed by "(-)." This notation is used only in the cutting columns for trimming two triangles using the S45. This tool has matched rulings on either side of a midline marked "0." Sometimes a patch will fall between the lines when it is centered. It is still easy to position the ruler correctly over the patch. The actual measurement would be slightly smaller than the measurement listed, which is why the listed measurement is followed by a "(-)." You simply place the listed measurement slightly outside the patch, with the space between the patch and rule line matching on both sides of the patch.

WHAT ABOUT SEAM ALLOWANCES?

The seam allowances included in the cutting dimensions are ¼" all around. It is common practice in rotary cutting to round numbers as long as we are talking about no more than a thread's width or thereabouts. When a patch's exact cutting dimensions could not be found on a ruler, I rounded the number where suitable. In some instances, however, the rounded number would be too inaccurate for reasonably precise patchwork. In such a case, I opted not to include the patch size.

WHAT IF THE SIZE I WANT IS NOT LISTED?

Sometimes, you will find the patch size you desire if you look in a chart for a different cutting method. If you don't find your desired size on any chart, you may want to resize your block so the patches can all be rotary cut. Magic Measures (page 22) usually work nicely. Or you can use a plastic template or a paper pattern taped to your ruler to cut the odd-sized patch.

HOW DO I CONVERT YIELD TO YARDAGE?

Figure yardage as follows: Make a list of patch shapes and sizes to be cut from each fabric in the quilt. Count the number of patches of one shape, size, and color in the quilt. Divide the number of patches by the number of patches per yard from the yield column in the chart. The result is the number of yards needed to cut the desired patch.

$$\frac{\#patches}{\#\ per\ yd.} = \#\ yards$$

Figure the yardages separately for each shape and size listed for one fabric. Add these yardages for different shapes and sizes of the same fabric together for the yardage total for the first fabric. Add a little extra for insurance. Repeat this procedure for each fabric in the quilt.

SQUARES

The square is the easiest shape to cut and sew. It is nearly always cut with its side on the straight grain. You need to know only one of the finished dimensions of the square: either its side or its diagonal. Both dimensions are given to help you size neighboring patches in the quilt block.

Diagonal Squares. When a square is tilted on the diagonal in the block, its diagonal is the most readily measured dimension. You can easily cut this kind of square using your regular ruler if you use one of the Magic Measures sizes (having nice numbers for side and diagonal). These sizes are included in the chart on the facing page.

Large Squares. In order to cut large squares, you may need to use a big square ruler and cut a single square at a time. For some squares, you may be able to cut the strip using two rulers (page 20). Some of the larger squares may be inefficient to cut from 18" strips. If you want lengthwise strips for these, choose a strip length from which you can cut squares without waste. For example, you might cut 10½" squares from a 22"-long strip.

A. finished side

B. finished diagonal

straight grain

CUTTING DIRECTIONS

C. Find your chosen square listed in the Description columns of the chart on the facing page. You may identify the square based on either its finished side or finished diagonal dimension. Follow the line listing your square size to the right for cutting directions and yield. Find the strip width in Column C of the Cutting box. Cut a strip in the listed width, either 18" or 44" long.

D. For a clean cut and a perfectly squared end, trim a sliver off the short end of the strip at a right angle to the long side. (Trim the left end for right handers; the right end for left handers.) Measure from the clean-cut end, and parallel subcut a square (page 14), aligning the measurement listed in Column D with the trimmed end, and cutting parallel to it on the ruler's edge. This makes a square.

Continue cutting squares as shown in D2.

C. Cut strip width.

D1. Cut square.

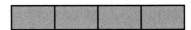

D2. Continue cutting strip into squares.

#S1: SQUARES

Description		Cutting		Yield (Yardage)					
				18" strips			44" strips		
A. fin. side	B. fin. diag- onal	C. cut strip width	D. cut square	# per strip	# per yard		# per strip	# per yard	
⅞"	1¼"	1⅜"	1⅜"	12	696		29	725	
1"	1⅜+	1½"	1½"	11	572		26	598	
1+	1½"	1½+	1½+	11	550		25	550	
1¼"	1¾"	1¾"	1¾"	10	440		22	440	
1⅜+	2"	1⅞+	1⅞+	9	360		20	360	
1½"	2⅛"	2"	2"	8	320		20	340	
1¾"	2½"	2¼"	2¼"	7	238		17	255	
2"	2¾+	2½"	2½"	7	224		16	224	
2⅛"	3"	2⅝"	2⅝"	6	180		15	195	
2½"	3½"	3"	3"	5	130		13	143	
2¾+	4"	3¼+	3¼+	5	120		12	120	
3"	4¼"	3½"	3½"	5	110		11	110	
3⅛+	4½"	3⅝+	3⅝+	4	80		10	90	
3½"	4⅞+	4"	4"	4	80		10	80	
3⅝"	5⅛"	4⅛"	4⅛"	4	72		9	72	
4"	5⅝+	4½"	4½"	3	48		8	56	
4¼"	6"	4¾"	4¾"	3	48		8	56	
4½"	6⅜"	5"	5"	3	48		8	56	
4⅞+	7"	5⅜+	5⅜+	3	42		7	42	
5"	7+	5½"	5½"	3	42		7	42	
5⅛"	7¼"	5⅝"	5⅝"	3	42		7	42	
6"	8½"	6½"	6½"	2	24		6	30	
6⅜"	9"	6⅞"	6⅞"	2	20		5	25	
7"	9⅞"	7½"	7½"	2	20		5	20	
7+	10"	7½+	7½+	2	20		5	20	
7¼"	10¼"	7¾"	7¾"	2	20		5	20	
7½"	10⅝"	8"	8"	2	20		5	20	
8"	11¼+	8½"	8½"	2	16		4	16	
8½"	12"	9"	9"	1	8		4	12	
9"	12¾"	9½"	9½"	1	8		4	12	
10"	14⅛"	10½"	10½"	1	6		3	9	
10¼"	14½"	10¾"	10¾"	1	6		3	9	
12"	17"	12½"	12½"	1	6		3	6	
14"	19¾+	14½"	14½"	1	4		2	4	

+   Cutting dimensions followed by "+" can be cut in the size listed using the black edge of the Rotaruler 16. If you prefer an ordinary rotary ruler, cut halfway between the listed number and the next larger one-eighth inch.

RECTANGLES

The rectangle is cut with its sides on the straight grain. Lengthwise strips will yield the long sides on the lengthwise grain. Crosswise strips will yield the short sides on the lengthwise grain. Lengthwise strips are clearly more desirable here. You need to know two finished dimensions of the rectangle: both its short and long sides. Rectangles are arranged by charts according to the relationship of the finished long side to the finished short side. The Rectangles for Sashes Chart on page 33 helps you cut sashes for the most common block sizes.

Log Cabins. The Rectangle Charts on pages 29–32 are perfect for Log Cabin blocks. For successively larger logs in the block, choose the same strip width and progress through each chart for the rectangle lengths.

Tilted Rectangles. When a rectangle is tilted on the diagonal in the block, you can easily cut it using your regular ruler. Determine the rectangle's side dimensions based on the patches next to it in the block (page 22).

Long Rectangles. Some of the longer rectangles may be inefficient to cut from 18" strips. If you want lengthwise strips for these, choose a strip length from which you can cut rectangles without waste. For example, you might cut 10½"-long rectangles from a 22"-long strip cut from ⅝ yard of fabric.

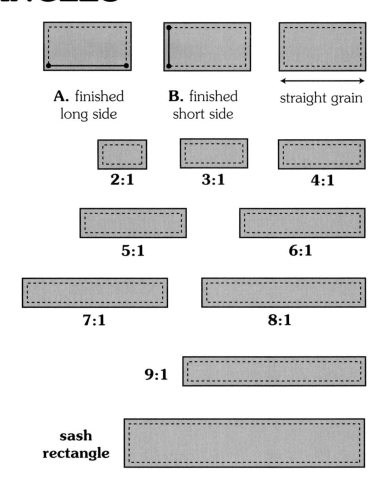

A. finished long side

B. finished short side

straight grain

2:1 3:1 4:1

5:1 6:1

7:1 8:1

9:1

sash rectangle

CUTTING DIRECTIONS FOR ALL RECTANGLES

C. Find your chosen rectangle listed in the Description columns of the charts that follow. Follow the line listing your rectangle's finished length and width to the right for cutting directions and yield. Find the strip width in Column C of the Cutting box. Cut a strip in the listed width, either 18" or 44" long.

D. For a clean cut and a perfectly squared end, trim a sliver off the short end of the strip, at a right angle to the long side. (Trim the left end for right handers; the right end for left handers.) Measure from the clean-cut end and parallel subcut (page 14) a rectangle, aligning the measurement listed in Column D with the trimmed end, and cutting parallel to it on the ruler's edge. This makes a rectangle.

Continue cutting rectangles as shown.

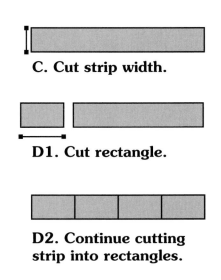

C. Cut strip width.

D1. Cut rectangle.

D2. Continue cutting strip into rectangles.

#S2: RECTANGLES (2:1)

Description		Cutting		Yield (Yardage)				
				18" strips		44" strips		
A. fin. long side	B. fin. short side	C. cut strip width	D. cut rec-tangle	# per strip	# per yard	# per strip	# per yard	
1¾"	⅞"	1⅜"	2¼"	7	406	16	400
2"	1"	1½"	2½"	7	364	16	368
2⅛"	1+	1½+	2⅝"	6	300	14	308
2½"	1¼"	1¾"	3"	5	220	12	240
2¾+	1⅜+	1⅞+	3¼+	5	200	12	216
3"	1½"	2"	3½"	5	200	10	170
3½"	1¾"	2¼"	4"	4	136	10	150
4"	2"	2½"	4½"	3	96	8	112
4¼"	2⅛"	2⅝"	4¾"	3	90	8	104
5"	2½"	3"	5½"	3	78	6	66
5⅝+	2¾+	3¼+	6⅛+	2	48	6	60
6"	3"	3½"	6½"	2	44	6	60

+ Cutting dimensions followed by "+" can be cut in the size listed using the black edge of the Rotaruler 16. If you prefer an ordinary rotary ruler, cut halfway between the listed number and the next larger one-eighth inch.

#S3: RECTANGLES (3:1)

Description		Cutting		Yield (Yardage)				
				18" strips		44" strips		
A. fin. long side	B. fin. short side	C. cut strip width	D. cut rec-tangle	# per strip	# per yard	# per strip	# per yard	
2⅝"	⅞"	1⅜"	3⅛"	5	290	12	300
3"	1"	1½"	3½"	5	260	10	230
3⅛+	1+	1½+	3⅝+	4	200	10	220
3¾"	1¼"	1¾"	4¼"	4	176	8	160
4¼"	1⅜+	1⅞+	4¾"	3	120	8	144
4½"	1½"	2"	5"	3	120	8	136
5¼"	1¾"	2¼"	5¾"	3	102	6	90
6"	2"	2½"	6½"	2	64	6	84
6⅜"	2⅛"	2⅝"	6⅞"	2	60	4	52
7½"	2½"	3"	8"	2	52	4	44
8½"	2¾+	3¼+	9"	1	24	4	40
9"	3"	3½"	9½"	1	22	4	40

+ Cutting dimensions followed by "+" can be cut in the size listed using the black edge of the Rotaruler 16. If you prefer an ordinary rotary ruler, cut halfway between the listed number and the next larger one-eighth inch.

#S4: RECTANGLES (4:1)

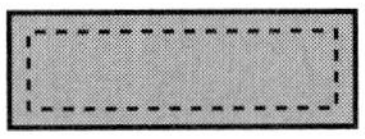

Description		Cutting		Yield (Yardage)					
				18" strips				44" strips	
A. fin. long side	B. fin. short side	C. cut strip width	D. cut rec- tangle	# per strip	# per yard			# per strip	# per yard
3½"	⅞"	1⅜"	4"	4	232			10	250
4"	1"	1½"	4½"	3	156			8	184
4¼"	1+	1½+	4¾"	3	150			8	176
5"	1¼"	1¾"	5½"	3	132			6	120
5⅝+	1⅜+	1⅞+	6⅛+	2	80			6	108
6"	1½"	2"	6½"	2	80			6	102
7"	1¾"	2¼"	7½"	2	68			4	60
8"	2"	2½"	8½"	2	64			4	56

+   Cutting dimensions followed by "+" can be cut in the size listed using the black edge of the Rotaruler 16. If you prefer an ordinary rotary ruler, cut halfway between the listed number and the next larger one-eighth inch.

#S5: RECTANGLES (5:1)

Description		Cutting		Yield (Yardage)					
				18" strips				44" strips	
A. fin. long side	B. fin. short side	C. cut strip width	D. cut rec- tangle	# per strip	# per yard			# per strip	# per yard
4⅜"	⅞"	1⅜"	4⅞"	3	174			8	200
5"	1"	1½"	5½"	3	156			6	138
5¼+	1+	1½+	5¾+	3	150			6	132
6¼"	1¼"	1¾"	6¾"	2	88			4	80
7+	1⅜+	1⅞+	7½+	2	80			4	72
7½"	1½"	2"	8"	2	80			4	68
8¾"	1¾"	2¼"	9¼"	1	34			4	60
10"	2"	2½"	10½"	1	32			3	42

+   Cutting dimensions followed by "+" can be cut in the size listed using the black edge of the Rotaruler 16. If you prefer an ordinary rotary ruler, cut halfway between the listed number and the next larger one-eighth inch.

30

#S6: RECTANGLES (6:1)

Description		Cutting		Yield (Yardage)				
A. fin. long side	B. fin. short side	C. cut strip width	D. cut rec- tangle	18" strips		44" strips		
				# per strip	# per yard	# per strip	# per yard	
5¼"	⅞"	1⅜"	5¾"	3	174	6	150	
6"	1"	1½"	6½"	2	104	6	138	
6⅜"	1+	1½+	6⅞"	2	100	4	88	
7½"	1¼"	1¾"	8"	2	88	4	80	
8½"	1⅜+	1⅞+	9"	1	40	4	72	
9"	1½"	2"	9½"	1	40	4	68	
10½"	1¾"	2¼"	11"	1	34	3	45	
12"	2"	2½"	12½"	1	32	3	42	

+   Cutting dimensions followed by "+" can be cut in the size listed using the black edge of the Rotaruler 16. If you prefer an ordinary rotary ruler, cut halfway between the listed number and the next larger one-eighth inch.

#S7: RECTANGLES (7:1)

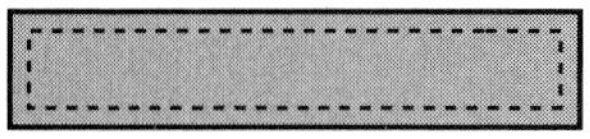

Description		Cutting		Yield (Yardage)				
A. fin. long side	B. fin. short side	C. cut strip width	D. cut rec- tangle	18" strips		44" strips		
				# per strip	# per yard	# per strip	# per yard	
6⅛"	⅞"	1⅜"	6⅝"	2	116	6	150	
7"	1"	1½"	7½"	2	104	4	92	
7⅜+	1+	1½+	7⅞+	2	100	4	88	
8¾"	1¼"	1¾"	9¼"	1	44	4	80	
9⅞"	1⅜+	1⅞+	10⅜"	1	40	3	54	
10½"	1½"	2"	11"	1	40	3	51	
12¼"	1¾"	2¼"	12¾"	1	34	3	45	
14"	2"	2½"	14½"	1	32	2	28	

+   Cutting dimensions followed by "+" can be cut in the size listed using the black edge of the Rotaruler 16. If you prefer an ordinary rotary ruler, cut halfway between the listed number and the next larger one-eighth inch.

#S8: RECTANGLES (8:1)

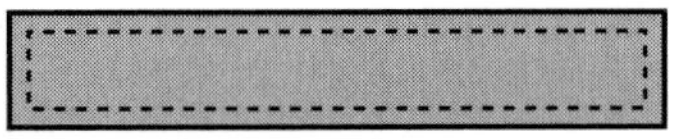

Description		Cutting		Yield (Yardage)					
				18" strips			44" strips		
A. fin. long side	B. fin. short side	C. cut strip width	D. cut rec-tangle	# per strip	# per yard		# per strip	# per yard	
7"	⅞"	1⅜"	7½"	2	116		4	100	
8"	1"	1½"	8½"	2	104		4	92	
8½"	1+	1½+	9"	1	50		4	88	
10"	1¼"	1¾"	10½"	1	44		3	60	
11¼+	1⅜+	1⅞+	11¾+	1	40		3	54	
12"	1½"	2"	12½"	1	40		3	51	
14"	1¾"	2¼"	14½"	1	34		2	30	
16"	2"	2½"	16½"	1	32		2	28	

+ Cutting dimensions followed by "+" can be cut in the size listed using the black edge of the Rotaruler 16. If you prefer an ordinary rotary ruler, cut halfway between the listed number and the next larger one-eighth inch.

#S9: RECTANGLES (9:1)

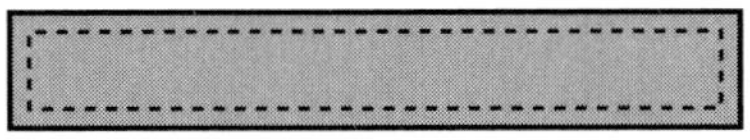

Description		Cutting		Yield (Yardage)					
				18" strips			44" strips		
A. fin. long side	B. fin. short side	C. cut strip width	D. cut rec-tangle	# per strip	# per yard		# per strip	# per yard	
7⅞"	⅞"	1⅜"	8⅜"	2	116		4	100	
9"	1"	1½"	9½"	1	52		4	92	
9½+	1+	1½+	10+	1	50		3	66	
11¼"	1¼"	1¾"	11¾"	1	44		3	60	
12¾"	1⅜+	1⅞+	13¼"	1	40		3	54	
13½"	1½"	2"	14"	1	40		2	34	
15¾"	1¾"	2¼"	16¼"	1	34		2	30	
18"	2"	2½"	18½"	0	0		2	28	

+ Cutting dimensions followed by "+" can be cut in the size listed using the black edge of the Rotaruler 16. If you prefer an ordinary rotary ruler, cut halfway between the listed number and the next larger one-eighth inch.

#S10: RECTANGLES FOR SASHES

Description		Cutting		Yield (Yardage)					
				18" strips				44" strips	
A. fin. long side	B. fin. short side	C. cut strip width	D. cut rec-tangle	# per strip	# per yard			# per strip	# per yard
8"	1"	1½"	8½"	2	104			4	92
8"	2"	2½"	8½"	2	64			4	56
8½"	1¼"	1¾"	9"	1	44			4	80
8½"	1¾"	2¼"	9"	1	34			4	60
8½"	2⅛"	2⅝"	9"	1	30			4	52
8½"	2½"	3"	9"	1	26			4	44
8½"	3½"	4"	9"	1	20			4	32
9"	1"	1½"	9½"	1	52			4	92
9"	1⅛"	1⅝"	9½"	1	48			4	84
9"	1½"	2"	9½"	1	40			4	68
9"	2¼"	2¾"	9½"	1	28			4	48
9"	3"	3½"	9½"	1	22			4	40
10"	1"	1½"	10½"	1	52			3	69
10"	1¼"	1¾"	10½"	1	44			3	60
10"	2"	2½"	10½"	1	32			3	42
10"	2½"	3"	10½"	1	26			3	33
10¼"	2⅛"	2⅝"	10¾"	1	30			3	39
10¼"	2½+	3+	10¾"	1	26			3	33
10¼"	3"	3½"	10¾"	1	22			3	30
12"	1"	1½"	12½"	1	52			3	69
12"	1½"	2"	12½"	1	40			3	51
12"	2"	2½"	12½"	1	32			3	42
12"	3"	3½"	12½"	1	22			3	30
14"	1"	1½"	14½"	1	52			2	46
14"	1¾"	2¼"	14½"	1	34			2	30
14"	2"	2½"	14½"	1	32			2	28
14"	3½"	4"	14½"	1	20			2	16

+ Cutting dimensions followed by "+" can be cut in the size listed using the black edge of the Rotaruler 16. If you prefer an ordinary rotary ruler, cut halfway between the listed number and the next larger one-eighth inch.

HALF-SQUARE TRIANGLES

The isosceles right triangle is the main triangle used in quiltmaking. It has two equal sides and a right angle.

Shortcuts. There are many shortcuts (as well as detours) for making this shape. I discuss the pros and cons of a few of these methods on pages 10–12. For most methods, the dimensions and yields listed here will be useful. However, the dimensions differ, and you will need nearly twice the fabric listed here if you plan to cut a single triangle from a square. My personal choice is to always cut triangles from stacked fabric as described here or on page 36. These methods offer complete flexibility for scrap quilts, and they actually save time in the long run. Besides, they are the only rotary cutting methods that will work for some common patchwork blocks, such as the LeMoyne Star or Hands All 'Round.

Point Trimming. It is usually helpful to trim the excess from the seam allowances at the points of this shape. You can easily do this with a Point Trimmer tool. Trims of three kinds are available. Choose the kind that will help you align patches for sewing. If you will be trimming the points parallel to the short sides of the triangle, you will save strokes and time by cutting pre-trimmed triangles using the chart on page 36 or 37 instead of using the chart on page 35 and then trimming.

Large Sizes. Your ruler may not be wide enough to cut some of the strip widths listed in Column C. For these larger sizes, use a big square ruler to cut one square at a time. For some triangles, you may be able to cut the strip using two rulers (page 20).

Switching Grains. Sometimes, you may want to cut a half-square triangle to substitute for a quarter-square triangle. The shapes are the same, but the grains are different. Identify the triangle size by the finished long side. (You can look this up in the quarter-square triangles chart on page 39 if you know the cut size of the square to be quartered.) Then find the same finished side in the half-square triangle chart on page 35, 36, or 37, and cut as directed. You will be able to switch grains and still use a regular ruler for many sizes, including the Magic Measures.

A. finished short side

A. finished short side

B. finished long side

straight grain

CUTTING DIRECTIONS

C. Find your chosen size listed in the Description columns of the chart on the facing page. You may identify the triangle based on either its finished long side or finished short side. Follow the line listing your triangle size to the right for cutting directions and yield. Find Column C, the strip width. Cut a strip in the listed width, either 18" or 44" long.

D. Trim off a sliver to square up the short end of the strip at a right angle to the long edge. (Trim the left end for right handers, the right end for left handers.) Parallel subcut a square (page 14), aligning the measurement listed in Column D with the trimmed end and cutting parallel to it on the ruler's edge. This makes a square.

E. Cut the square in half along the diagonal (refer to page 15) to complete two triangles.

Continue subcutting the strip into squares and cutting each square into two triangles as shown in Figure E2.

C. Cut strip width.

D. Cut square.

E. Cut square in half diagonally.

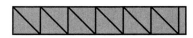
E2. Continue cutting this way.

#T1: HALF-SQUARE TRIANGLES

Description		Cutting		E.	Yield (Yardage)			
A. fin. short side	B. fin. long side	C. cut strip width	D. cut square	cut in half diagonally to make two triangles	18" strips		44" strips	
					# per strip	# per yard	# per strip	# per yard
⅞"	1¼"	1¾"	1¾"		20	880	44	880
1"	1⅜+	1⅞"	1⅞"		18	756	42	756
1+	1½"	1⅞+	1⅞+		18	720	40	720
1¼"	1¾"	2⅛"	2⅛"		16	576	36	576
1⅜+	2"	2¼"	2¼"		14	476	34	510
1½"	2⅛"	2⅜"	2⅜"		14	448	32	448
1¾"	2½"	2⅝"	2⅝"		12	360	30	390
2"	2¾+	2⅞"	2⅞"		12	312	26	312
2⅛"	3"	3"	3"		10	260	26	286
2½"	3½"	3⅜"	3⅜"		10	220	22	220
2¾+	4"	3⅝+	3⅝+		8	160	20	180
3"	4¼"	3⅞"	3⅞"		8	160	20	180
3⅛+	4½"	4+	4+		8	144	18	144
3½"	4⅞+	4⅜"	4⅜"		8	144	18	144
3⅝"	5⅛"	4½"	4½"		6	96	16	112
4"	5⅝+	4⅞"	4⅞"		6	96	16	112
4¼"	6"	5⅛"	5⅛"		6	84	14	84
4½"	6⅜"	5⅜"	5⅜"		6	84	14	84
4⅞+	7"	5¾+	5¾+		6	72	12	72
5"	7+	5⅞"	5⅞"		4	48	12	60
5⅛"	7¼"	6"	6"		4	48	12	60
5½"	7¾"	6⅜"	6⅜"		4	48	12	60
5⅝+	8"	6½"	6½"		4	48	12	60
6"	8½"	6⅞"	6⅞"		4	40	10	50
6⅜"	9"	7¼"	7¼"		4	40	10	40
6½"	9⅛+	7⅜"	7⅜"		4	40	10	40
7+	10"	7⅞+	7⅞+		4	40	10	40
7¼"	10¼"	8⅛"	8⅛"		4	32	8	32
7½"	10⅝"	8⅜"	8⅜"		4	32	8	32
8"	11¼+	8⅞"	8⅞"		2	16	8	24
8½"	12"	9⅜"	9⅜"		2	16	8	24
9"	12¾"	9⅞"	9⅞"		2	16	8	24
10"	14⅛"	10⅞"	10⅞"		2	12	6	18
10¼"	14½"	11⅛"	11⅛"		2	12	6	18
12"	17"	12⅞"	12⅞"		2	12	6	12

+   Cut sizes followed by "+" using the black edge of the Rotaruler 16. Or use an ordinary rotary ruler, cutting halfway between the listed number and the next larger ⅛".

PRETRIMMED "HALF-SQUARE" TRIANGLES

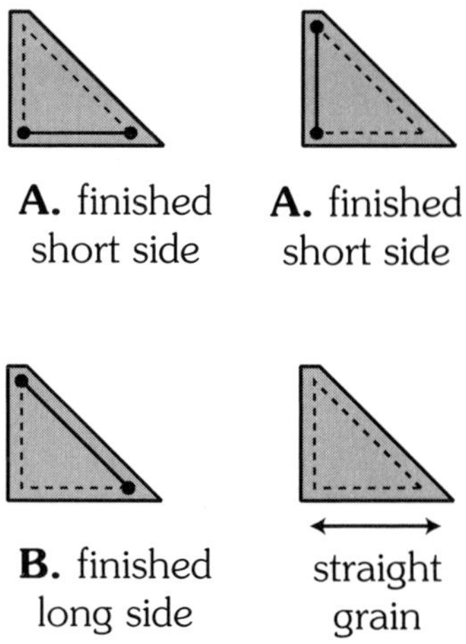

This is the same finished triangle as the one on pages 34–35. With the method described here, triangles can be cut from the same strips used to cut squares. Rather than subcutting the strip into squares, you cut it into triangles. You will need a Shapemaker 45 tool or an Omnigrid® triangle #96 or 96L. The S45 will give you any size, in ⅛" increments, up to 5". The Omnigrid® will give you any size, in ½" increments, up to 6" (#96) or 8" (#96L). Use the chart below with the S45 and the chart facing with Omnigrid® tools. See page 17 for more details on using the Omnigrid® tool.

A. finished short side   **A.** finished short side

When Do I Use This Method? Use this method for triangles with points trimmed as shown at right. When you want to trim the points to reduce bulk in the seam allowances or to help you align patches for sewing, this cutting method is the most efficient one. In no more strokes than it takes to cut ordinary half-square triangles, you can cut the same size triangles with one point of each already trimmed. Use a Point Trimmer to easily trim the second point to match the first. If you don't have a Point Trimmer, you can use a ruler to trim the remaining point, as follows. Leave triangles neatly stacked. Align the ruling listed in Column C over the short edge of the triangle, opposite the remaining point. The point should extend about ⅜" beyond the ruler. Cut along the ruler's edge to trim off the point.

B. finished long side   straight grain

Large Sizes. A 6½"- or 7"-wide ruler is wide enough to cut strips for all but the three or four biggest triangles in these charts. If your ruler is too narrow for your desired triangle size, use two rulers together to measure and cut strips.

#T2: PRETRIMMED TRIANGLES USING S45

Description		Cutting			Yield (Yardage)			
A. fin. short side	B. fin. long side	C. cut strip width	D. cut triangle (S45)	E. cut triangle (reg.)	18" strips		44" strips	
					# per strip	# per yard	# per strip	# per yard
⅞"	1¼"	1⅜"	1¾"	1¾"	16	928	36	900
1"	1⅜+	1½"	1⅞"	1⅞"	14	728	34	782
1¼"	1¾"	1¾"	2⅛"	2⅛"	14	616	32	640
1½"	2⅛"	2"	2⅜"	2⅜"	12	480	28	476
1¾"	2½"	2¼"	2⅝"	2⅝"	10	340	26	390
2"	2¾+	2½"	2⅞"	2⅞"	10	320	24	336
2⅛"	3"	2⅝"	3"	3"	10	300	22	286
2½"	3½"	3"	3⅜"	3⅜"	8	208	20	220
3"	4¼"	3½"	3⅞"	3⅞"	8	176	18	180
3½"	4⅞+	4"	4⅜"	4⅜"	6	120	16	128
4"	5⅝+	4½"	4⅞"	4⅞"	6	96	14	98
4¼"	6"	4¾"	5⅛"	5⅛"	6	96	14	98
4½"	6⅜"	5"	5⅜"	5⅜"	6	96	12	84
5"	7+	5½"	5⅞"	5⅞"	4	56	12	72

+   For finished dimensions followed by "+," add ¹⁄₁₆" to the listed number.

CUTTING DIRECTIONS

C. In the chart for your tool, find the line listing your triangle size and follow it to the right for cutting directions and yield. Find Column C, the strip width. Use a regular ruler to cut a strip in the listed width, 18" or 44" long.

C. Cut strip width.

D. Trim off a sliver to square up the short end of the strip at a right angle to the long edge. (Trim the left end for right handers; the right end for left handers.) Use the Shapemaker 45 or the Omnigrid® triangle #96 or 96L to cut a triangle.

For the S45 method, align the measurement listed in Column D (page 36) with the trimmed end, and align the base of the tool with the long edge of the strip. Cut along the angled short side of the S45 to make a triangle.

For the Omnigrid® method, align the line for the size listed in Column D (below) with the end of the strip and align the short side of the ruler with the base of the strip. Cut along the angled long side of the Omnigrid® tool.

D. Use the S45 to 45° subcut a triangle or use the Omnigrid® triangle.

E. For the S45 method, use a regular ruler to right angle subcut the next triangle (page 15.) To do so, align the ruling listed in E (page 36) with the strip's point. Align the strip's long edge with any ruling that crosses the first ruling. Cut along the long edge of the ruler to make a second triangle.

For the Omnigrid® method, turn the triangle tool and align its long edge with the angled cut and the top of the strip with the line listed in column E below. Cut along the short side of the tool to complete a second triangle.

Continue subcutting the strip into triangles as shown in Figure E2.

E. Use a regular ruler to right angle subcut a triangle (S45 method) or use the Omnigrid® triangle tool.

E2. Continue cutting this way, alternating D and E steps.

#T3: PRETRIMMED TRIANGLES USING OMNIGRID®

Description		Cutting			Yield (Yardage)			
					18" strips		44" strips	
A. fin. short side	B. fin. long side	C. cut strip width	D. cut triangle Omni	E. cut triangle Omni	# per strip	# per yard	# per strip	# per yard
1"	1⅜+	1½"	1"	1"	14	728	34	782
1½"	2⅛"	2"	1½"	1½"	12	480	28	476
2"	2¾+	2½"	2"	2"	10	320	24	336
2½"	3½"	3"	2½"	2½"	8	208	20	220
3"	4¼"	3½"	3"	3"	8	176	18	180
3½"	4⅞+	4"	3½"	3½"	6	120	16	128
4"	5⅝+	4½"	4"	4"	6	96	14	98
4½"	6⅜"	5"	4½"	4½"	6	96	12	84
5"	7+	5½"	5"	5"	4	56	12	72
5½"	7¾"	6"	5½"	5½"	4	48	10	50
6"	8½"	6½"	6"	6"	4	48	10	50
6½"	9⅛+	7"	6½"	6½"	4	40	10	50
7"	9⅞"	7½"	7"	7"	4	40	8	32
7½"	10⅝"	8"	7½"	7½"	4	40	8	32
8"	11¼+	8½"	8"	8"	2	16	8	32

+ For finished dimensions followed by "+," add ¹⁄₁₆ to the listed number.

QUARTER-SQUARE TRIANGLES

The isosceles right triangle is the main triangle used in quiltmaking. It has two equal sides and a right angle. It can be cut with straight grain on the short side (pages 34–37) or on the long side (pages 38–42). There are several ways to cut the same triangle.

Comparison of Methods. The usual method for cutting these triangles with the long side on the straight grain is the Quarter-Square Triangles method described here. I prefer the Triangle Strips methods on pages 40–42 because they yield triangles that are all on the same grain. The Quarter-Square Triangles method yields half of the triangles on the lengthwise grain and half on the crosswise grain. Quarter-square triangles must be cut along both diagonals, which means you must be careful to keep the triangles perfectly in place after the first diagonal cut. There is only one diagonal cut for the Triangle Strips methods. Another advantage of the Triangle Strips method is that the strips are half as wide and, therefore, more readily cut.

Point Trimming. It is usually helpful to trim the excess from the seam allowances at the points of this shape. Usually points are trimmed down to ¼" at right angles to the long side. This kind of trim is most easily done with a Point Trimmer tool. Depending on your block, you may need to use one of the other trim types instead, as explained in the tool instructions.

Large Sizes. Your ruler may not be wide enough to cut some of the strip widths listed in Column C. For these larger sizes, use a big square ruler to cut one square at a time; use two rulers together (page 20); or use the Triangle Strips method on the following pages.

A. finished long side

B. finished short side

B. finished short side

straight grain

CUTTING DIRECTIONS

C. Find your chosen size listed in the Description columns of the chart on the facing page. You may identify the triangle based on either its finished long side or finished short side. Follow the line listing your triangle size to the right for cutting directions and yield. Find Column C, the strip width. Cut a strip in the listed width, either 18" or 44" long.

D. Trim off a sliver to square up the short end of the strip at a right angle to the long edge. (Trim the left end for right handers; the right end for left handers.) Parallel subcut (page 14) a square, aligning the measurement listed in Column D with the trimmed end, and cutting parallel to it on the ruler's edge. This makes a square.

E. Cut the square in half along the diagonal (page 15) to make two triangles. Keep the triangles in place exactly in a square, and cut along the other diagonal to complete four triangles.

Continue subcutting the strip into squares and cutting each square into four triangles as shown in Figure E2.

C. Cut strip width.

D. Cut square.

E. Cut square in half along both diagonals.

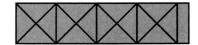

E2. Continue cutting this way.

#T4: QUARTER-SQUARE TRIANGLES

Description		Cutting			Yield (Yardage)			
A. fin. long side	B. fin. short side	C. cut strip width	D. cut square	E. cut square along both diagonals to make four triangles	18" strips		44" strips	
					# per strip	# per yard	# per strip	# per yard
1¼"	⅞"	2½"	2½"		28	896	64	896
1⅜+	1"	2⅝"	2⅝"		24	720	60	780
1½"	1+	2¾"	2¾"		24	672	56	672
1¾"	1¼"	3"	3"		20	520	52	572
2"	1⅜+	3¼"	3¼"		20	480	48	480
2⅛"	1½"	3⅜"	3⅜"		20	440	44	440
2½"	1¾"	3¾"	3¾"		16	320	40	360
2¾+	2"	4+	4+		16	288	36	288
3"	2⅛"	4¼"	4¼"		16	288	36	288
3½"	2½"	4¾"	4¾"		12	192	32	224
4"	2¾+	5¼"	5¼"		12	168	28	168
4¼"	3"	5½"	5½"		12	168	28	168
4½"	3⅛+	5¾"	5¾"		12	144	24	144
4⅞+	3½"	6⅛+	6⅛+		8	96	24	120
5"	3½+	6¼"	6¼"		8	96	24	120
5⅛"	3⅝"	6⅜"	6⅜"		8	96	24	120
5½"	3⅞"	6¾"	6¾"		8	80	20	100
5⅝+	4"	6⅞"	6⅞"		8	80	20	100
6"	4¼"	7¼"	7¼"		8	80	20	80
6⅜"	4½"	7⅝"	7⅝"		8	80	20	80
6½"	4⅝"	7¾"	7¾"		8	80	20	80
7"	4⅞+	8¼"	8¼"		8	64	16	64
7+	5"	8¼+	8¼+		8	64	16	64
7¼"	5⅛"	8½"	8½"		8	64	16	64
7½"	5¼+	8¾"	8¾"		8	64	16	64
7¾"	5½"	9"	9"		4	32	16	48
8"	5⅝+	9¼"	9¼"		4	32	16	48
8½"	6"	9¾"	9¾"		4	32	16	48
9"	6⅜"	10¼"	10¼"		4	24	12	36
9⅛+	6½"	10⅜"	10⅜"		4	24	12	36
9⅞"	7"	11⅛"	11⅛"		4	24	12	36
10"	7+	11¼"	11¼"		4	24	12	36
10¼"	7¼"	11½"	11½"		4	24	12	36
10⅝"	7½"	11¾+	11¾+		4	24	12	24

+ Cutting dimensions followed by "+" can be cut in the size listed using the black edge of the Rotaruler 16. If you prefer an ordinary rotary ruler, cut halfway between the listed number and the next larger one-eighth inch.

39

TRIANGLE STRIPS

The Triangle Strips method is a better way to cut the isosceles right triangle on page 38. Here, the long side is always on the same straight grain. See the comparison of methods as well as the notes on large sizes and point trimming on page 38. Depending on your desired triangle size and your tools on hand, you can cut triangle strips using the Shapemaker 45, Omnigrid® Triangles 98 or 98L, or the Quilter's Rule™ Triangles QR-T6 or QR-T12, as described in the next few pages. (See page 17 for more about the tools.)

The S45 method will cut triangles in ⅛" increments with the long side up to 8¾" long. The Omnigrid® method will cut triangles in ½" increments with the long side up to 12" long. The Quilter's Rule™ method will cut triangles in ½" increments with the *short* side up to 12" long. The S45 can be used for triangles based on their long or short sides. The Omnigrid® method is for triangles of a known long side. The Quilter's Rule™ method is useful for triangles based on their short sides, though the long side is on the straight grain.

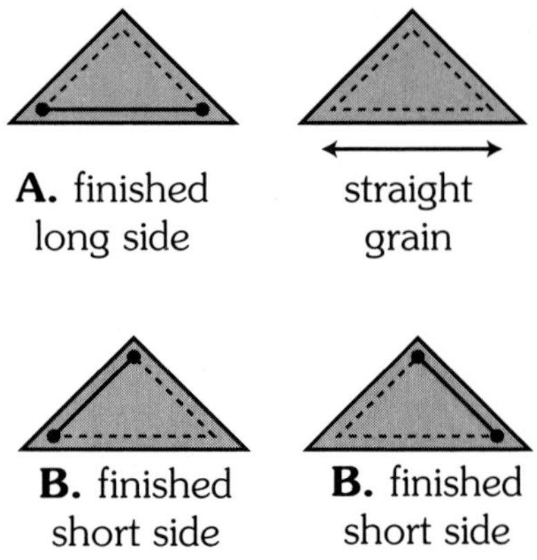

A. finished long side   straight grain

B. finished short side   **B.** finished short side

#T5: TRIANGLE STRIPS USING OMNIGRID® TRIANGLES

Description		Cutting			Yield (Yardage)			
					18" strips		**44" strips**	
A. fin. long side	B. fin. short side	C. cut strip width	D. cut angle 45°	E. cut triangle	# per strip	# per yard	# per strip	# per yard
1"	⅝+	1⅛"		1"	14	980	32	992
1½"	1+	1⅜"		1½"	11	638	28	700
2"	1⅜+	1⅝"		2"	9	432	23	483
2½"	1¾	1⅞"		2½"	8	336	20	360
3"	2⅛	2⅛"		3"	7	252	17	272
3½"	2½	2⅜"		3½"	6	192	15	210
4"	2¾+	2⅝"		4"	5	150	14	182
4½"	3⅛+	2⅞"		4½"	5	130	12	144
5"	3½+	3⅛"		5"	4	96	11	121
5½"	3⅞	3⅜"		5½"	4	88	10	100
6"	4¼	3⅝"		6"	3	66	10	90
6½"	4⅝	3⅞"		6½"	3	60	9	81
7"	4⅞+	4⅛"		7"	3	54	8	64
7½"	5¼+	4⅜"		7½"	3	54	8	64
8"	5⅝+	4⅝"		8"	2	32	7	49
8½"	6	4⅞"		8½"	2	32	7	49
9"	6⅜	5⅛"		9"	2	28	6	36
9½"	6⅝+	5⅜"		9½"	2	28	6	36
10"	7+	5⅝"		10"	2	28	6	36
10½"	7⅜+	5⅞"		10½"	1	12	5	25
11"	7¾	6⅛"		11"	1	12	5	25
11½"	8⅛	6⅜"		11½"	1	12	5	25
12"	8½	6⅝"		12"	1	12	5	25

+   For finished dimensions followed by "+," add 1⁄16" to the listed number.

CUTTING DIRECTIONS

C. Find your chosen size in one of the charts on pages 40–42. Follow the line to the right to Column C, the strip width. Use a regular ruler to cut a strip in the listed width, either 18" or 44" long.

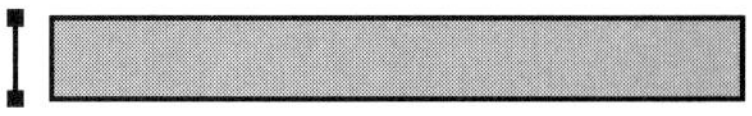

D. Trim off the lower left corner of the strip at a 45° angle. (Left handers trim off the lower right corner.)

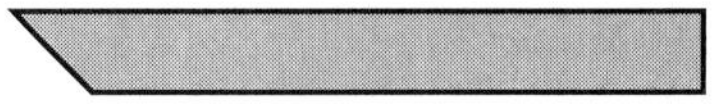

E. Use the Omnigrid® Triangle, the Shapemaker 45 tool, or the Quilter's Rule™ Triangle to subcut a triangle. To do this with the S45, align the long edge of the tool with the long side of the strip and align the measurement listed in Column E with the point of the strip. With the other two tools, align the cutting line for the listed size with the long side of the strip. Align the short side with the angled end. For all tools, cut along the tool's short edge to complete a triangle. Turn the tool to cut the next triangle. Read more about the tools on page 17.

Continue subcutting the strip into triangles as shown in Figure E2.

C. Cut strip width.

D. Trim end at 45° angle.

E. Use the S45, or the Omnigrid®, or Quilter's Rule™ triangle tool to cut off a triangle.

E2. Continue cutting this way.

#T6: TRIANGLE STRIPS USING SHAPEMAKER 45

Description		Cutting			Yield (Yardage)			
A. fin. long side	**B. fin. short side**	**C. cut strip width**	**D. cut angle 45°**	**E. cut triangle**	**18" strips**		**44" strips**	
					# per strip	**# per yard**	**# per strip**	**# per yard**
1"	⅝+	1⅛"		2¼"	14	980	32	992
1¼"	⅞"	1¼"		2½"	13	832	31	868
1½"	1+	1⅜"		2¾"	11	638	28	700
1¾"	1¼"	1½"		3"	10	520	25	575
2"	1⅜+	1⅝"		3¼"	9	432	23	483
2⅛"	1½"	1⅝+		3⅜"	9	414	22	440
2½"	1¾"	1⅞"		3¾"	8	336	20	360
3"	2⅛"	2⅛"		4¼"	7	252	17	272
3½"	2½"	2⅜"		4¾"	6	192	15	210
4"	2¾+	2⅝"		5¼"	5	150	14	182
4¼"	3"	2¾"		5½"	5	140	13	156
4½"	3⅛+	2⅞"		5¾"	5	130	12	144
5"	3½+	3⅛"		6¼"	4	96	11	121
5⅛"	3⅝"	3⅛+		6⅜"	4	96	11	110
5½"	3⅞"	3⅜"		6¾"	4	88	10	100
6"	4¼"	3⅝"		7¼"	3	66	10	90
6⅜"	4½"	3¾+		7⅝"	3	60	9	81
6½"	4⅝"	3⅞"		7¾"	3	60	9	81
7"	4⅞+	4⅛"		8¼"	3	54	8	64
7¼"	5⅛"	4¼"		8½"	3	54	8	64
7½"	5¼+	4⅜"		8¾"	3	54	8	64
8"	5⅝+	4⅝"		9¼"	2	32	7	49
8½"	6"	4⅞"		9¾"	2	32	7	49

+ See note below chart on page 39.

MORE TRIANGLE STRIPS
#T7: TRIANGLE STRIPS USING QUILTER'S RULE™

Description		Cutting			Yield (Yardage)			
A. fin. long side	B. fin. short side	C. cut strip width	D. cut angle 45°	E. cut triangle	18" strips		44" strips	
					# per strip	# per yard	# per strip	# per yard
1⅜+	1"	1¼+		1"	12	720	29	754
2⅛"	1½"	1⅝+		1½"	9	414	22	440
2¾+	2"	2"		2"	7	280	18	306
3½"	2½"	2⅜"		2½"	6	192	15	210
4¼"	3"	2¾"		3"	5	140	13	156
4⅞+	3½"	3+		3½"	4	96	11	121
5⅝+	4"	3⅜+		4"	4	88	10	100
6⅜"	4½"	3¾+		4½"	3	60	9	81
7+	5"	4⅛"		5"	3	54	8	64
7¾"	5½"	4½"		5½"	2	32	7	49
8½"	6"	4⅞"		6"	2	32	7	49
9⅛+	6½"	5¼"		6½"	2	28	6	36
9⅞"	7"	5½+		7"	2	28	6	36
10⅝"	7½"	5⅞"		7½"	1	12	5	25
11¼+	8"	6¼"		8"	1	12	5	25
12"	8½"	6⅝"		8½"	1	12	5	25
12¾"	9"	7"		9"	1	10	4	20
13⅜+	9½"	7¼+		9½"	1	10	4	16
14⅛"	10"	7⅝+		10"	1	10	4	16
14⅞"	10½"	8"		10½"	1	10	3	12
15½+	11"	8⅜"		11"	1	8	3	12
16¼"	11½"	8¾"		11½"	1	8	3	12
17"	12"	9⅛"		12"	0	0	3	9

+ Cutting dimensions followed by "+" can be cut in the size listed using the black edge of the Rotaruler 16. If you prefer an ordinary rotary ruler, cut halfway between the listed number and the next larger one-eighth inch.

See the description, cutting directions, and figures on the previous two pages.

45° HALF DIAMOND TRIANGLES

If you cut this shape from folded fabric the grain will run along one A side for half the patches and the other A side for the other half. Two of these triangles joined along their short sides make a 45° diamond. This shape is often used with 45° diamonds (page 50) or the triangles on pages 44–45.

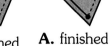

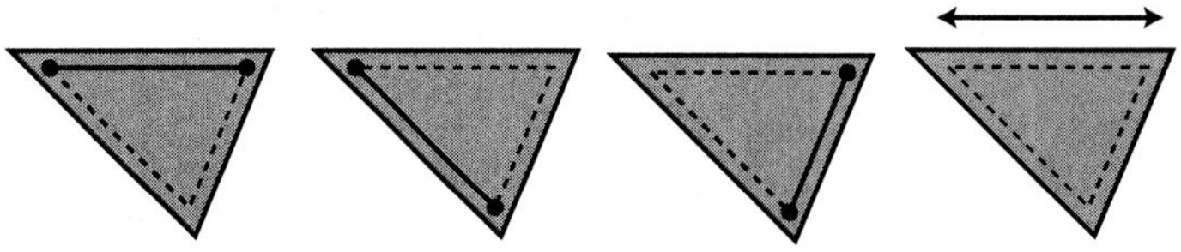

A. finished long side **A.** finished long side **B.** finished short side straight grain

CUTTING DIRECTIONS

C. Find your chosen size listed in the Description columns of the chart below. You may identify the triangle based on either its finished long side or finished short side. Follow the line listing your triangle size to the right for cutting directions and yield. Find the strip width in Column C of the Cutting box. Cut a strip in the listed width, either 18" or 44" long.

D. Cut off the lower left corner at a 45° angle.

E. Cut a diamond by making a parallel subcut (page 14). That is, lay the ruling listed in Column E along the angled end of the strip and cut along the ruler's edge.

F. Cut the diamond in half diagonally to make two triangles (page 15). Continue cutting diamonds and triangles as shown. Discard the last triangle of the strip if it runs off the edge.

C. Cut strip width.

D. Cut off end at 45° angle.

E. Measure from angled end and cut diamond.

 F. Cut diamond in half diagonally.

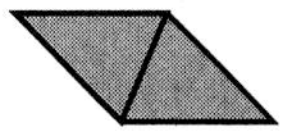

F2. Continue cutting this way.

#T8: 45° HALF DIAMOND TRIANGLES

Description		Cutting				Yield (Yardage)			
A. fin. long side	**B. fin. short side**	**C. cut strip width**	**D. cut angle 45°**	**E. cut dia-mond**	**F. cut in half diagonally**	**18" strips**		**44" strips**	
						# per strip	**# per yard**	**# per strip**	**# per yard**
1¼"	⅞+	1½+		1½+		14	700	34	748
1½"	1⅛"	1¾"		1¾"		13	572	31	620
1¾"	1¼+	1⅞+		1⅞+		11	440	27	486
2"	1½+	2⅛"		2⅛"		10	360	24	384
2⅛"	1⅝+	2⅜+		2⅜+		10	360	22	352
3"	2¼+	2¾+		2¾+		7	196	18	216
3½"	2⅝+	3⅛+		3⅛+		6	144	14	140
4¼"	3¼"	3⅝+		3⅝+		5	100	13	117
4½"	3⅜+	3⅞"		3⅞"		5	100	11	99
5"	3¾+	4¼"		4¼"		4	72	10	80
6"	4½+	4⅞+		4⅞+		3	48	9	63

+ Cutting dimensions followed by "+" can be cut in the size listed using the black edge of the Rotaruler 16. If you prefer an ordinary rotary ruler, cut halfway between the listed number and the next larger one-eighth inch.

45°-22½°-112½° TRIANGLES

This triangle is found in many 4- or 8-pointed stars. It is often used with the triangles on pages 43 and 45. Folded fabric yields mirror images.

CUTTING DIRECTIONS

E. Find your chosen size listed in the Description columns of the chart below. Follow the line listing your triangle size to the right to Column E, the strip width. Cut a strip in the listed width, either 18" or 44" long.

F. Trim off the lower left corner (the lower right corner for left handers) of the strip at a 45° angle.

G. Subcut parallel (page 14) to the angled end, aligning the measurement listed in Column G with the trimmed end, and cutting parallel to it on the ruler's edge. This makes a parallelogram.

H. Cut the parallelogram in half along the diagonal (page 15) to make two triangles.
    Continue subcutting the strip into paralellograms and cutting each in half to make triangles as shown in Figure H2.

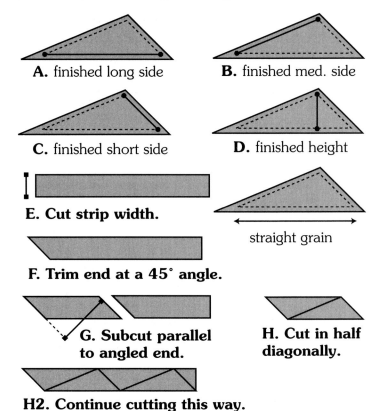

A. finished long side

B. finished med. side

C. finished short side

D. finished height

E. Cut strip width.

straight grain

F. Trim end at a 45° angle.

G. Subcut parallel to angled end.

H. Cut in half diagonally.

H2. Continue cutting this way.

#T9: 45°-22½°-112½° TRIANGLES

Description				Cutting				Yield (Yardage)			
								18" strips		44" strips	
A. fin. long side	B. fin. med. side	C. fin. short side	D. fin. height	E. cut strip width	F. cut angle 45°	G. cut paral-lelo-gram	H. cut in ½ diagonally into 2 triangles	# per strip	# per yard	# per strip	# per yard
2"	1½"	¾+	½+	1⅛"		2¾"		8	560	19	589
2⅛"	1⅝"	⅞"	⅝"	1⅛+		2¾+		8	528	18	522
2½"	1⅞+	1+	¾"	1¼+		3+		7	420	17	442
3"	2¼+	1¼"	⅞"	1⅜+		3⅜+		6	324	16	384
3⅜+	2⅝"	1⅜+	1"	1½+		3¾"		6	300	14	308
3⅝"	2¾"	1½"	1+	1⅝"		3⅞"		6	288	13	273
4"	3+	1⅝+	1⅛+	1¾"		4⅛+		4	176	12	240
4¼"	3¼"	1¾"	1¼"	1¾+		4¼+		4	176	12	228
4½"	3⅜+	1⅞"	1¼+	1⅞"		4½"		4	168	11	198
5"	3¾"	2+	1⅜+	2"		4⅞"		4	160	10	170
5⅛"	3⅞"	2⅛"	1½"	2+		4⅞+		4	152	10	160
6"	4½+	2½"	1¾"	2¼+		5½+		3	102	9	135
6⅜"	4⅞	2⅝"	1⅞"	2⅜+		5¾+		3	96	8	112

+   Cutting dimensions followed by "+" can be cut in the size listed using the black edge of the Rotaruler 16. If you prefer an ordinary rotary ruler, cut halfway between the listed number and the next larger one-eighth inch.

22½°-67½°-90° TRIANGLES

This triangle is found in many 4- or 8-pointed stars. It is often used with the triangles on pages 43 and 44. Folded fabric yields mirror images.

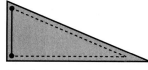

A. finished med. side

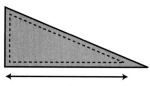

B. finished short side

CUTTING DIRECTIONS

D. Find your chosen size listed in the Description columns of the chart below. Follow the line listing your triangle size to the right to Column D, the strip width. Cut a strip in the listed width, either 18" or 44" long.

E. Cut a sliver off the short end at a right angle to the long sides. (Trim the left end for right handers; the right end for left handers.) Subcut parallel (page 14) to this trimmed end, aligning the measurement listed in Column E with the end, and cutting parallel to it on the ruler's edge. This makes a rectangle.

F. Cut the rectangle in half along the diagonal (page 15) to make two triangles.

Continue subcutting the strip into rectangles and cutting each in half to make triangles as shown in Figure F2.

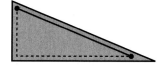

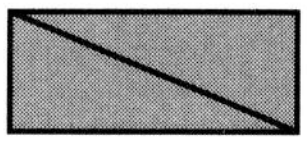

C. finished long side

straight grain

D. Cut strip width.

E. Subcut a rectangle.

F. Cut in half diagonally to make 2 triangles.

F2. Continue cutting this way.

#T10: 22½°-67½°-90° TRIANGLES

Description			Cutting			Yield (Yardage)			
A. fin. med. side	**B. fin. short side**	**C. fin. long side**	**D. cut strip width**	**E. cut rec- tangle**	**F.** cut in half diagonally	18" strips		44" strips	
						# per strip	**# per yard**	**# per strip**	**# per yard**
2"	¾+	2⅛+	1⅜+	3½"		10	540	22	528
2⅛"	⅞"	2¼+	1½"	3⅝"		8	416	22	506
2⅜+	1"	2⅝"	1⅝"	3⅞+		8	384	20	420
2½+	1+	2¾"	1⅝+	4+		8	368	18	360
3"	1¼"	3¼"	1⅞"	4½"		6	252	16	288
3⅛+	1¼+	3⅜+	1⅞+	4⅝+		6	240	16	288
3⅝"	1½"	3⅞+	2⅛"	5⅛"		6	216	14	224
4¼"	1¾"	4⅝"	2⅜"	5¾"		6	192	12	168
4½"	1⅞"	4⅞"	2½"	6"		4	128	12	168
4¾+	2"	5⅛+	2⅝"	6¼+		4	120	12	156
6"	2½"	6½"	3⅛"	7½"		4	96	10	110

+ Cutting dimensions followed by "+" can be cut in the size listed using the black edge of the Rotaruler 16. If you prefer an ordinary rotary ruler, cut halfway between the listed number and the next larger one-eighth inch.

30°-60°-90° TRIANGLES

This triangle is found in many patterns involving hexagons or equilateral (60°) triangles. It is often used to square off the edges of a block or quilt made using 60° patches. Other shapes in this family are on pages 47, 54, and 55. Note that folded fabric yields mirror images.

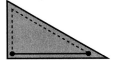
A. finished med. side

B. finished short side

CUTTING DIRECTIONS

D. Find your chosen size listed in the Description columns of the chart below. Follow the line listing your triangle size to the right to Column D, the strip width. Cut a strip in the listed width, either 18" or 44" long.

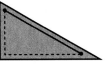
C. finished long side

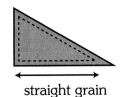
straight grain

D. Cut strip width.

E. Cut a sliver off the short end at a right angle to the long sides. (Right handers trim the left end; left handers trim the right end.) Subcut parallel (page 14) to this trimmed end, aligning the measurement listed in Column E with the end, and cutting parallel to it on the ruler's edge. This makes a rectangle.

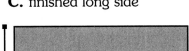
E. Parallel subcut a rectangle.

F. Cut the rectangle in half along the diagonal (page 15) to make two triangles.

Continue subcutting the strip into rectangles and cutting each in half to make triangles as shown in Figure F2.

F. Cut in half diagonally to make 2 triangles.

F2. Continue cutting this way.

#T11: 30°-60°-90° TRIANGLES

Description			Cutting			Yield (Yardage)			
A. fin. med. side	B. fin. short side	C. fin. long side	D. cut strip width	E. cut rec-tangle	F. cut in half diagonally	18" strips		44" strips	
						# per strip	# per yard	# per strip	# per yard
1½"	⅞"	1¾"	1½+	2⅝+		12	600	28	616
1¾"	1"	2"	1⅝+	2⅞+		10	460	26	520
2"	1⅛"	2¼+	1¾+	3⅛+		10	440	24	456
2½"	1⅜+	2⅞"	2⅛"	3⅝+		8	288	20	320
3"	1¾"	3½"	2⅜+	4⅛+		8	256	18	252
4"	2¼+	4⅝"	3"	5⅛+		6	156	14	154
5"	2⅞"	5¾"	3½+	6⅛+		4	88	12	108
6"	3⅜+	6⅞+	4⅛"	7⅛+		4	72	10	80

+ Cutting dimensions followed by "+" can be cut in the size listed using the black edge of the Rotaruler 16. If you prefer an ordinary rotary ruler, cut halfway between the listed number and the next larger one-eighth inch.

60° (EQUILATERAL) TRIANGLES

This triangle is found in Thousand Pyramids as well as many hexagon-shaped blocks. It is proportioned with three equal sides and three equal angles. The 60° triangle is often used with the shapes on pages 46, 54, and 55.

 A. finished height 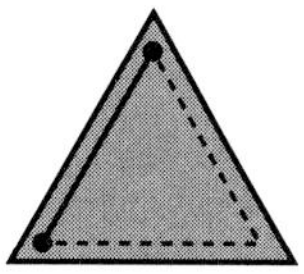 **B.** finished side 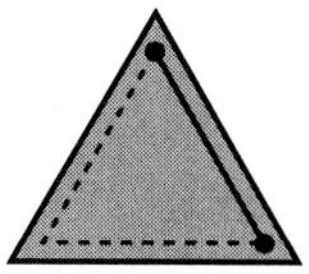 **B.** finished side 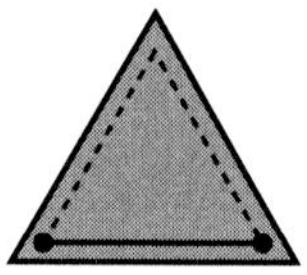 **B.** finished side

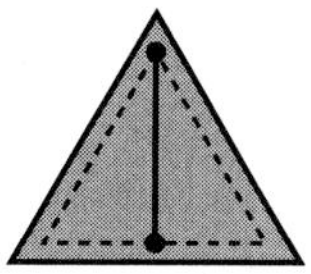

CUTTING DIRECTIONS

C. Find your chosen size listed in the Description columns of the chart below. Follow the line listing your triangle size to the right to Column C, the strip width. Cut a strip in the listed width, either 18" or 44" long.

C. Cut strip width.

D. Cut a triangle off the lower left corner (lower right corner for left handers) at a 60° angle.

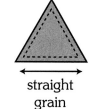

straight grain

D. Cut off end at a 60° angle.

E. Subcut parallel (page 14) to this trimmed end, aligning the measurement listed in Column E with the end, and cutting parallel to it on the ruler's edge. This makes a diamond.

E. Subcut a diamond.

F. Cut the diamond in half along the diagonal (page 15) to make two triangles.

Continue subcutting diamonds and cutting each in half to make triangles as shown in Figure F2.

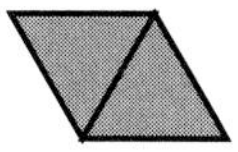

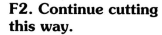

F. Cut in half diagonally to make 2 triangles.

F2. Continue cutting this way.

#T12: EQUILATERAL TRIANGLES (60°)

Description		Cutting				Yield (Yardage)			
						18" strips		44" strips	
A. fin. height	B. fin. side	C. cut strip width	D. cut angle 60°	E. cut dia-mond	F. cut in half to make two triangles	# per strip	# per yard	# per strip	# per yard
¾"	⅞"	1½"		1½"		19	988	44	1012
⅞"	1"	1⅝"		1⅝"		17	816	40	840
1"	1⅛"	1¾"		1¾"		16	704	36	720
1¼"	1⅜+	2"		2"		14	560	32	544
1½"	1¾"	2¼"		2¼"		12	408	28	420
1¾"	2"	2½"		2½"		11	352	24	336
2"	2¼+	2¾"		2¾"		10	280	22	264
2½"	2⅞"	3¼"		3¼"		8	192	18	180
3"	3⅜+	3¾"		3¾"		7	140	16	144
4"	4⅝"	4¾"		4¾"		5	80	12	84
5"	5¾"	5¾"		5¾"		4	48	10	60
6"	6⅞+	6¾"		6¾"		3	30	8	40

+ For finished dimensions followed by "+," add ¹⁄₁₆" to the listed number.

HALF-RECTANGLE TRIANGLES (2:1)

This triangle is sometimes called "spike" or "recs." It is often paired with the triangle (sometimes called "peaky" or "tri") on the following page or with the 90° kite on page 62. Specialty tools are available to cut this triangle in the most common sizes. The yields here should be pretty close to what the specialty tools will yield. Use the chart below if you do not have the specialty tools or if you want to cut this triangle in a size not available on the tools. Note that folded fabric yields mirror images.

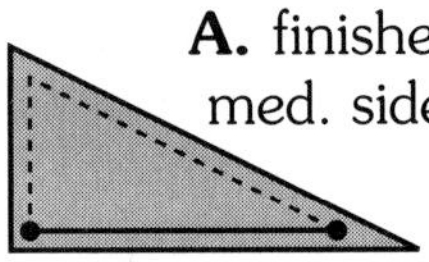

A. finished med. side 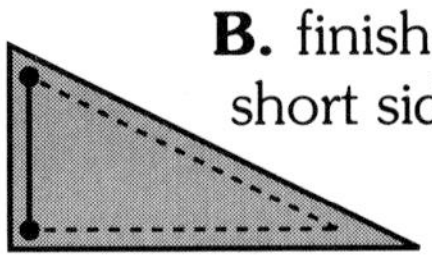   **B.** finished short side

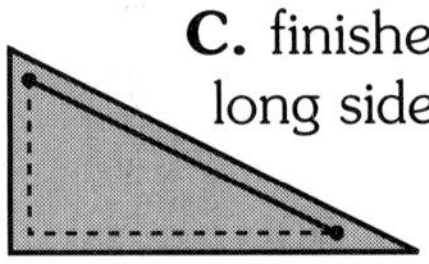

C. finished long side 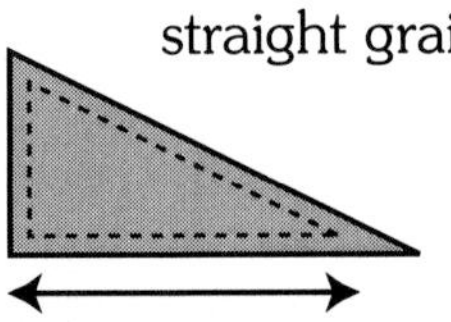   straight grain

CUTTING DIRECTIONS

D. Find your chosen size listed in the Description columns of the chart below. You may identify the triangle based on any of its finished sides. Follow the line listing your triangle size to the right to Column D, the strip width. Cut a double-size strip in the listed width, either 18" or 44" long.

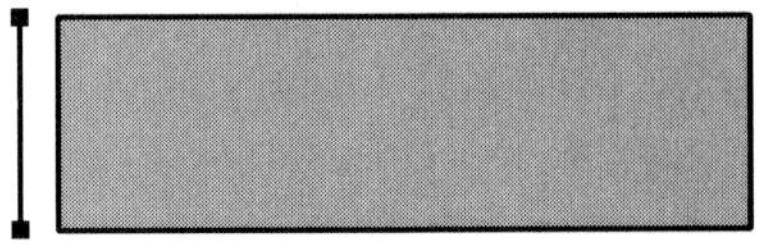

D. Cut strip width listed.

E. Crease the strip in half as shown. Iron the crease. Measure ⅛" from the crease and trim. This allows you to measure in 16ths and get a strip width in 32nds for perfect half-rectangle triangles.

E. Fold strip in half and trim ⅛" from fold.

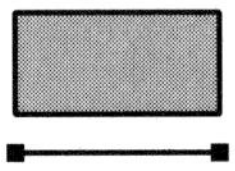

F. Cut a sliver off the short end at a right angle to the long sides of the strip. Subcut parallel (page 14) to this trimmed end, aligning the measurement listed in Column F with the end and cutting parallel to it. This makes two rectangles.

F. Cut rectangle.   **G. Cut in ½ diagonally.**

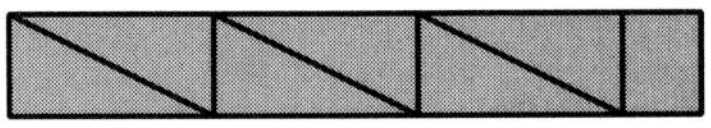

G. For mirror images, leave the two rectangles stacked and cut them in half diagonally to make four triangles. If you don't want mirror images, restack the rectangles so all layers are face up before cutting them in half.

Continue cutting rectangles and triangles from the strip, as shown in G2.

G2. Continue as shown.

#T13: HALF-RECTANGLE TRIANGLES (2:1)

Description			Cutting				Yield (Yardage)			
A. fin. med. side	**B. fin. short side**	**C. fin. long side**	**D. cut dbl. strip width**	**E. crease strip in ½, trim ⅛" from fold**	**F. cut rec-tangle**	**G. cut rectangle in half diagonally**	18" strips		44" strips	
							# per dbl. strip	# per yard	# per dbl. strip	# per yard
1¾"	⅞"	1⅞+	3¼+		3+		20	480	52	520
2"	1"	2¼"	3½+		3¼+		20	440	48	432
2½"	1¼"	2¾+	4+		3¾+		16	288	40	320
2¾+	1⅜+	3⅛+	4⅜"		4⅛"		16	288	36	288
3"	1½"	3⅜"	4½+		4¼+		16	256	36	252
3½"	1¾"	3⅞+	5+		4¾+		12	168	32	192
4"	2"	4½"	5½+		5¼+		12	168	28	168
4¼"	2⅛"	4¾"	5¾+		5½+		12	144	28	168
5"	2½"	5½+	6½+		6¼+		8	96	24	120
6"	3"	6⅝+	7½+		7¼+		8	80	20	80

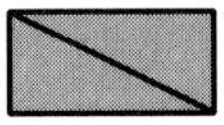

+ Cutting dimensions followed by "+" can be cut in the size listed using the black edge of the Rotaruler 16. If you prefer an ordinary rotary ruler, cut halfway between the listed number and the next larger one-eighth inch.

TRIANGLES OF EQUAL HEIGHT & WIDTH

This triangle is proportioned like two half-rectangle triangles joined together. It is sometimes known as "tri" or "peaky," and is often combined with the triangle on page 48 or the kite on page 62.

 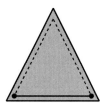 

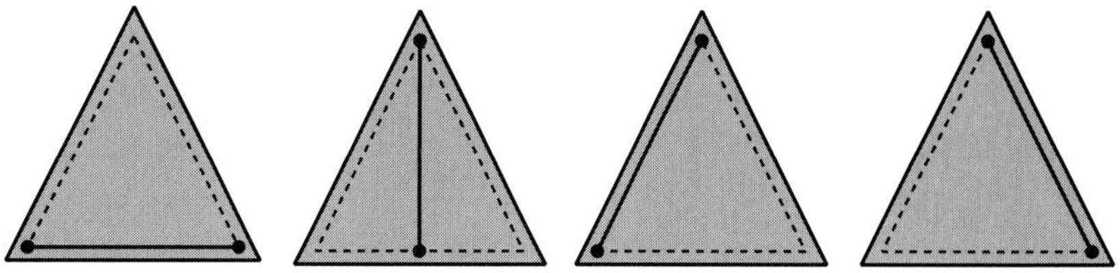

A. finished short side   **B.** finished height   **C.** finished long side   **C.** finished long side

CUTTING DIRECTIONS

D. Find your chosen size listed in the Description columns of the chart below. Follow the line listing your triangle size to the right to Column D, the strip width. Cut a strip in the listed width, either 18" or 44" long.

E. Cut off one end at a 2:1 angle as shown on page 16.

F. Subcut parallel (page 14) to this angled end, aligning the measurement listed in Column F with the end of the strip, and cutting parallel to it on the ruler's edge. This makes a parallelogram.

G. Cut the parallelogram in half along the diagonal (page 15) to make two triangles.

Continue subcutting the strip into parallelograms and cutting the parallelograms in half to make triangles as shown in Figure G2.

D. Cut strip width.

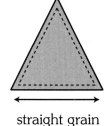

straight grain

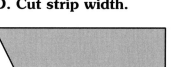

E. Cut off end at a 2:1 angle.

F. Subcut a parallelogram. 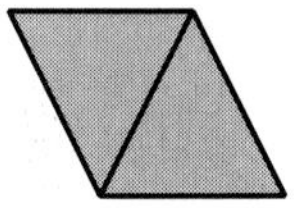   **G. Cut in half diagonally into 2 triangles.**

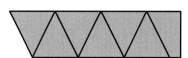

G2. Continue cutting this way.

#T14: TRIANGLES OF EQUAL HEIGHT & WIDTH

Description			Cutting				Yield (Yardage)			
A. fin. short side	**B. fin. height**	**C. fin. long side**	**D. cut strip width**	**E. cut angle 2:1 as shown on page 16**	**F. cut parallelogram**	**G. cut diagonally into 2 triangles**	18" strips		44" strips	
							# per strip	# per yard	# per strip	# per yard
1¾"	1¾"	1⅞+	2½+		2¼+		12	360	28	364
2"	2"	2¼"	2¾+		2½"		11	308	26	312
2⅛"	2⅛"	2⅜"	2⅞+		2⅝"		10	260	24	264
2½"	2½"	2¾+	3¼+		2⅞+		9	216	22	220
3"	3"	3⅜"	3¾+		3⅜+		8	160	18	162
3½"	3½"	3⅞+	4¼+		3⅞"		7	126	16	128
4"	4"	4½"	4¾+		4¼+		6	96	14	98
4¼"	4¼"	4¾"	5+		4½"		5	70	12	72
5"	5"	5½+	5¾+		5⅛+		5	60	10	60
6"	6"	6⅝+	6¾+		6+		4	40	8	40

+ Cutting dimensions followed by "+" can be cut in the size listed using the black edge of the Rotaruler 16. If you prefer an ordinary rotary ruler, cut halfway between the listed number and the next larger one-eighth inch.

45° DIAMONDS

The 45° diamond has four equal sides and angles of 45° and 135°. This is the diamond found in LeMoyne Stars, Lone Stars, and many other blocks. Although a diamond is not readily drawn on graph paper, it is no harder to sew than an uneven parallelogram and it makes a more elegant star. If you choose one of the sizes listed below, you can easily rotary cut the diamond, as well as the squares and triangles to fit with it, using your regular ruler. Compatible shapes are on pages 26, 34–43, 51, 56, and 57.

CUTTING DIRECTIONS

C. Find your chosen size listed in the Description columns of the chart below. You may identify the diamond based on either its finished side or finished width. Follow the line listing your diamond size to the right for cutting directions and yield. Find the strip width in Column C of the Cutting box. Cut a strip in the listed width, either 18" or 44" long.

D. Trim one short end of the strip at a 45° angle (page 14). (Trim off the lower left corner for right handers; the lower right corner for left handers.)

E. Measure from the angled end, and subcut the strip parallel to it (page 14) to make a diamond of the size listed in Column E.
Continue cutting diamonds as shown in Figure E2.

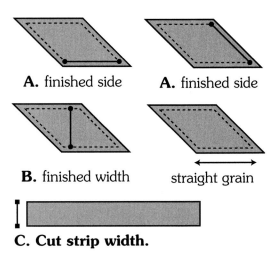

A. finished side   A. finished side

B. finished width   straight grain

C. Cut strip width.

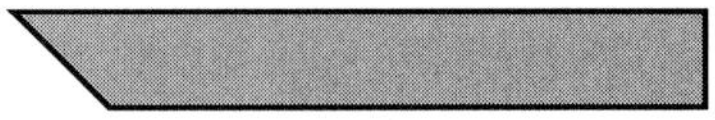

D. Cut off end at a 45° angle.

E. Subcut a diamond parallel to the angled end.

E2. Continue cutting this way.

#D1: 45° DIAMONDS

Description		Cutting			Yield (Yardage)			
					18" strips		44" strips	
A. fin. side	B. fin. width	C. cut strip width	D. cut angle 45°	E. cut diamond	# per strip	# per yard	# per strip	# per yard
1¼"	⅞"	1⅜"		1⅜"	8	464	18	450
1⅜+	1"	1½"		1½"	7	364	16	368
1½"	1+	1½+		1½+	7	350	16	352
1¾"	1¼"	1¾"		1¾"	6	264	14	280
2"	1⅜+	1⅞+		1⅞+	5	200	12	216
2⅛"	1½"	2"		2"	5	200	12	204
2½"	1¾"	2¼"		2¼"	4	136	10	150
2¾+	2"	2½"		2½"	4	128	10	140
3"	2⅛"	2⅝"		2⅝"	4	120	8	104
3⅛+	2¼"	2¾"		2¾"	3	84	8	96
3½"	2½"	3"		3"	3	78	8	88
3⅝"	2½+	3+		3+	3	78	8	88

+   See note below chart on facing page.

DOUBLE-DIAMOND PARALLELOGRAMS

This parallelogram is proportioned like two true 45° diamonds sewn end to end. It finishes with two sides that are twice as long as the other two sides. It is often used in combination with 45° diamonds (page 50). Note that folded fabric yields mirror images.

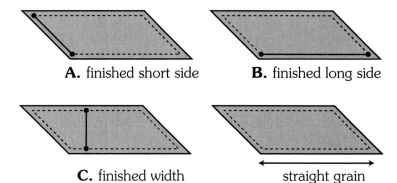

A. finished short side   **B.** finished long side

C. finished width   straight grain

CUTTING DIRECTIONS

D. Find your chosen size listed in the Description columns of the chart below. Follow the line listing your parallelogram size to the right to Column D, the strip width. Cut a strip in the listed width, either 18" or 44" long.

D. Cut strip width.

E. Trim off one short end of the strip at a 45° angle. (Right handers trim off the lower left corner; left handers trim off the lower right corner.)

E. Cut off end at a 45° angle.

F. Measure from the angled end of the strip, and subcut parallel to this angled end (page 14) to make a parallelogram of the size listed in Column F.

Continue cutting parallelograms as shown in F2.

F. Subcut a parallelogram.

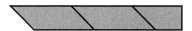

F2. Continue cutting this way.

#D2: 45° DOUBLE-DIAMOND PARALLELOGRAMS

Description			Cutting			Yield (Yardage)			
A. fin. short side	B. fin. long side	C. fin. width	D. cut strip width	E. cut angle 45°	F. cut parallelogram	18" strips		44" strips	
						# per strip	# per yard	# per strip	# per yard
1¼"	2½"	⅞"	1⅜"		2¼"	5	290	10	250
1⅜+	2¾+	1"	1½"		2½"	4	208	10	230
1½"	3"	1+	1½+		2⅝"	4	200	8	176
1¾"	3½"	1¼"	1¾"		3"	3	132	8	160
2⅛"	4¼"	1½"	2"		3½"	3	120	6	102
2½"	5"	1¾"	2¼"		4"	2	68	6	90
2¾+	5⅝+	2"	2½"		4½"	2	64	4	56
3"	6"	2⅛"	2⅝"		4¾"	2	60	4	52

+ Cutting dimensions followed by "+" can be cut in the size listed using the black edge of the Rotaruler 16. If you prefer an ordinary rotary ruler, cut halfway between the listed number and the next larger one-eighth inch.

PARALLELOGRAMS

This parallelogram is proportioned like two isosceles right triangles sewn head to foot. It is often used in grid-based blocks as a substitute for true diamonds. The parallelogram can be rotary cut with the short side on the straight grain, as shown on this page, or with the long side on the straight grain, shown on the facing page.

Mirror images. Cutting this shape from folded fabric will yield mirror images. If your pattern calls for all identical parallelograms, you must cut from unfolded fabrics. If you like, stack fabrics all facing the same way. If you want the shape shown here, the fabric should be face up. For the reverse of this image, fabric should be face down. Left handers can turn the fabric face down and cut from the right end to get the same patch shown here.

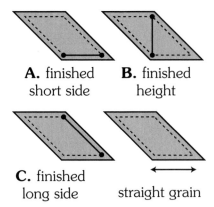

A. finished short side   B. finished height

C. finished long side   straight grain

D. Cut strip width.

CUTTING DIRECTIONS

D. Find your chosen size listed in the Description columns of the chart below. Follow the line listing your parallelogram size to the right to Column D, the strip width. Cut a strip in the listed width, either 18" or 44" long.

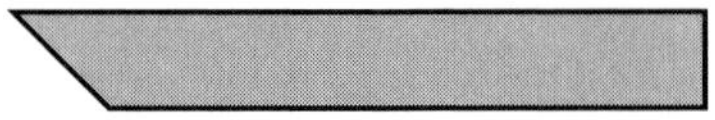

E. Cut off end at a 45° angle.

E. Trim one short end of the strip at a 45° angle. (Trim off the lower left corner for right handers; the lower right corner for left handers.)

F. Subcut a parallelogram.

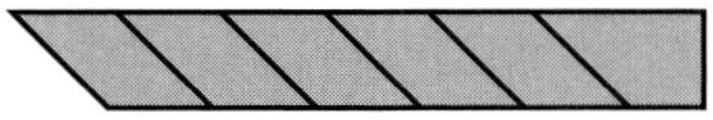

F. Measure from the angled end, and subcut the strip parallel to it (page 14) to make a parallelogram of the size listed in Column F.

Continue cutting parallelograms as shown in F2.

F2. Continue cutting this way.

#D3: PARALLELOGRAMS: SHORT SIDE STRAIGHT GRAIN

Description			Cutting			Yield (Yardage)			
						18" strips		44" strips	
A. fin. short side	B. fin. height	C. fin. long side	D. cut strip width	E. cut angle 45°	F. cut paral-lelo-gram	# per strip	# per yard	# per strip	# per yard
⅞"	⅞"	1¼"	1⅜"		1⅛"	10	580	22	550
1+	1+	1½"	1½+		1¼"	9	450	20	440
1¼"	1¼"	1¾"	1¾"		1⅜"	8	352	18	360
1⅜+	1⅜+	2"	1⅞+		1½"	7	280	16	288
1½"	1½"	2⅛"	2"		1½+	7	280	16	272
1¾"	1¾"	2½"	2¼"		1¾"	6	204	14	210
2"	2"	2¾+	2½"		1⅞+	5	160	12	168
2⅛"	2⅛"	3"	2⅝"		2"	5	150	12	156
2½"	2½"	3½"	3"		2¼"	4	104	10	110
2¾+	2¾+	4"	3¼+		2½"	4	96	8	80
3"	3"	4¼"	3½"		2⅝"	3	66	8	80

+ Cutting dimensions followed by "+" can be cut in the size listed using the black edge of the Rotaruler 16. If you prefer an ordinary rotary ruler, cut halfway between the listed number and the next larger one-eighth inch.

MORE PARALLELOGRAMS

This is the same parallelogram as the one on the facing page. The grain makes the difference. Here the straight grain is on the long side of the patch. The mirror-image note from the facing page applies here as well.

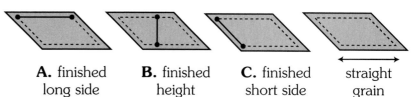

A. finished long side   **B.** finished height   **C.** finished short side   straight grain

CUTTING DIRECTIONS

D. Find your chosen size listed in the Description columns of the chart below. Follow the line listing your parallelogram size to the right to Column D, the strip width. Cut a strip in the listed width, either 18" or 44" long.

E. Trim one short end of the strip at a 45° angle. (Right handers trim off the lower left corner; left handers trim off the lower right corner.)

F. Measure from the angled end the distance listed in Column F, and subcut the strip parallel to this end (page 14). This makes a parallelogram.

Continue cutting parallelograms as shown in Figure F2.

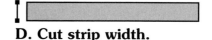

D. Cut strip width.

E. Cut off end at a 45° angle.

F. Subcut a parallelogram.

F2. Continue cutting this way.

#D4: PARALLELOGRAMS: LONG SIDE STRAIGHT GRAIN

Description			Cutting			Yield (Yardage)			
A. fin. long side	**B. fin. height**	**C. fin. short side**	**D. cut strip width**	**E. cut angle 45°**	**F. cut parallelogram**	**18" strips**		**44" strips**	
						# per strip	**# per yard**	**# per strip**	**# per yard**
1¼"	⅝"	⅞"	1⅛"		1⅜"	8	560	18	558
1½"	¾"	1+	1¼"		1½+	7	448	16	448
1¾"	⅞"	1¼"	1⅜"		1¾"	6	348	14	350
2"	1"	1⅜+	1½"		1⅞+	5	260	12	276
2⅛"	1+	1½"	1½+		2"	5	250	12	264
2½"	1¼"	1¾"	1¾"		2¼"	4	176	10	200
2¾+	1⅜+	2"	1⅞+		2½"	4	160	10	180
3"	1½"	2⅛"	2"		2⅝"	4	160	8	136
3½"	1¾"	2½"	2¼"		3"	3	102	8	120
4¼"	2⅛"	3"	2⅝"		3½"	3	90	6	78

+ Cutting dimensions followed by "+" can be cut in the size listed using the black edge of the Rotaruler 16. If you prefer an ordinary rotary ruler, cut halfway between the listed number and the next larger one-eighth inch.

60° DIAMONDS

This diamond has four equal sides and 60° and 120° angles. It is proportioned like two equilateral triangles sewn together. It is often used in hexagonal blocks. Related shapes are on pages 46, 47, and 55.

Mirror images. Cutting this shape from folded fabric yields two shapes the same, but with straight grain reversed on one. If your pattern is better with the grain the same for each diamond, you must cut from unfolded fabrics.

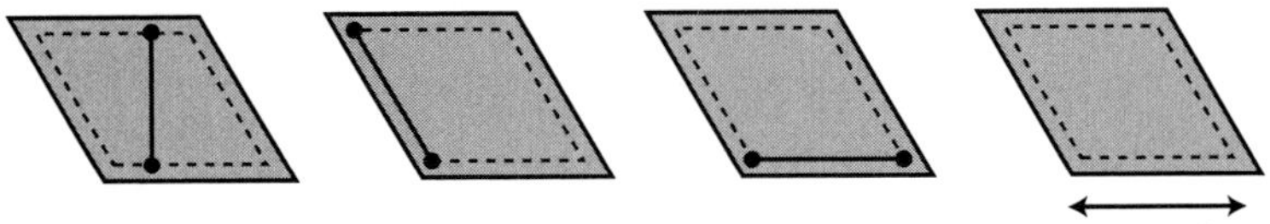

A. finished width   **B.** finished side   **B.** finished side   straight grain

CUTTING DIRECTIONS

C. Find your chosen diamond listed in the Description columns of the chart below. Follow the line listing your diamond size to the right to Column C, the strip width. Cut a strip in the listed width, either 18" or 44" long.

D. Trim off one short end of the strip at a 60° angle. (Right handers trim off the lower left corner; left handers trim off the lower right corner.)

E. Measure from the angled end, and subcut the strip parallel to it (page 14) to make a diamond of the size listed in Column E.

Continue cutting diamonds as shown in Figure E2.

C. Cut strip width.

D. Cut off end at a 60° angle.

E. Subcut a diamond.

E2. Continue cutting this way.

#D5: 60° DIAMONDS

Description		Cutting			Yield (Yardage)			
					18" strips		**44" strips**	
A. fin. width	**B. fin. side**	**C. cut strip width**	**D. cut angle 60°**	**E. cut dia-mond**	**# per strip**	**# per yard**	**# per strip**	**# per yard**
¾"	⅞"	1¼"		1¼"	11	704	26	728
⅞"	1"	1⅜"		1⅜"	10	580	24	600
1"	1⅛"	1½"		1½"	9	468	22	506
1¼"	1⅜+	1¾"		1¾"	8	352	18	360
1½"	1¾"	2"		2"	7	280	16	272
1¾"	2"	2¼"		2¼"	6	204	14	210
2"	2¼+	2½"		2½"	5	160	12	168
2½"	2⅞"	3"		3"	4	104	10	110
3"	3⅜+	3½"		3½"	3	66	8	80

+ Cutting dimensions followed by "+" can be cut in the size listed using the black edge of the Rotaruler 16. If you prefer an ordinary rotary ruler, cut halfway between the listed number and the next larger one-eighth inch.

HEXAGONS

The hexagon has six equal sides and 120° angles. It is proportioned like six equilateral triangles sewn together. It is used in Grandmother's Flower Garden and many other quilts. The hexagon is compatible with the 60° diamond on the facing page as well as the triangles on pages 46–47.

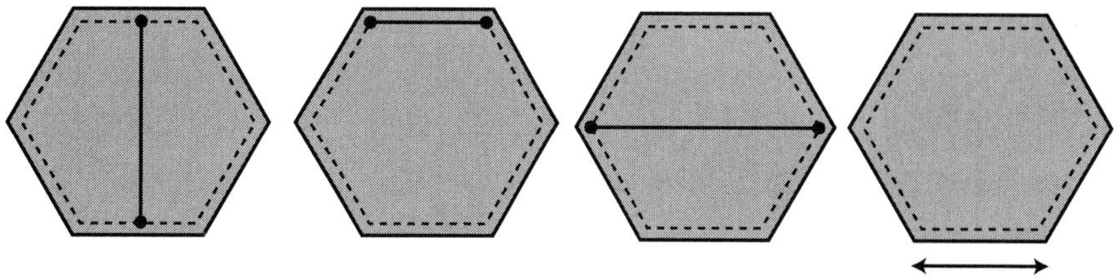

A. finished height **B.** finished side **C.** finished width straight grain

CUTTING DIRECTIONS

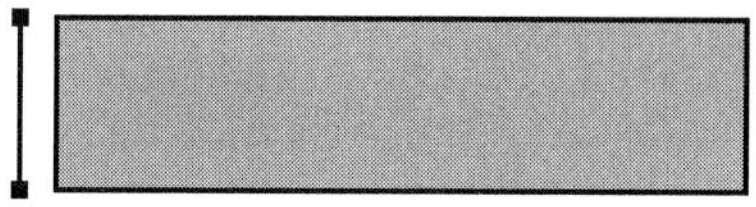

D. Cut strip width.

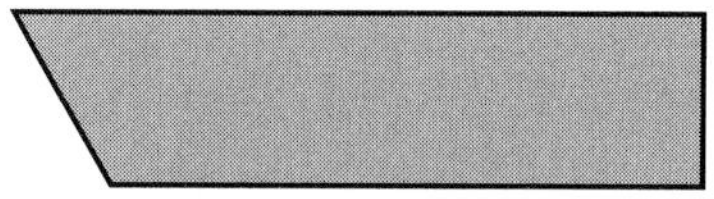

E. Cut off end at 60°

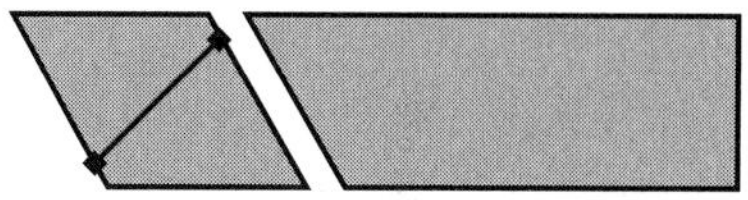

F. Subcut a diamond.

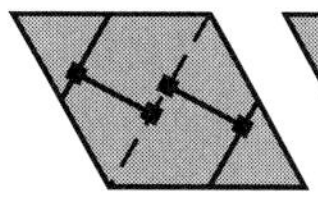

G. Cut parallel to diagonal on both sides.

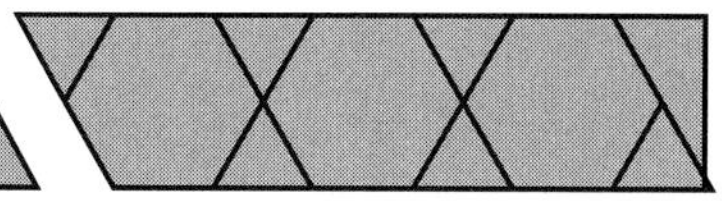

G2. Continue cutting this way.

D. Find your chosen size listed in the Description columns of the chart below. Follow the line listing your hexagon size to the right to Column D, the strip width. Cut a strip in the listed width, either 18" or 44" long.

E. Trim one short end of the strip at a 60° angle. (Trim off the lower left corner for right handers; trim off the lower right corner for left handers.)

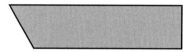

F. Measure from the angled end, and subcut the strip parallel to it (page 14) to make a diamond of the size listed in Column F.

G. Cut parallel to the diagonal (page 16) as follows. Lay the measurement listed in Column G from one corner of the diamond to the opposite corner and cut along the edge of the ruler. Repeat for the opposite side of the same diagonal. This completes a hexagon.

Continue cutting hexagons as shown in Figure G2.

#M1: HEXAGONS

Description			Cutting Dimensions				Yield (Yardage)			
							18" strips		44" strips	
A. fin. height	B. fin. side	C. fin. width	D. cut strip width	E. cut angle 60°	F. cut diamond	G. cut dist. from diag.	# per strip	# per yard	# per strip	# per yard
1"	½+	1⅛"	1½"		1½"	¾"	9	468	22	506
1½"	⅞"	1¾"	2"		2"	1"	7	280	16	272
1¾"	1"	2"	2¼"		2¼"	1⅛"	6	204	14	210
2"	1⅛"	2¼+	2½"		2½"	1¼"	5	160	12	168
2½"	1⅜+	2⅞"	3"		3"	1½"	4	104	10	110
3"	1¾"	3⅜+	3½"		3½"	1¾"	4	88	8	80
3½"	2"	4+	4"		4"	2"	3	60	8	64
4"	2¼+	4⅝"	4½"		4½"	2¼"	3	48	6	42
5"	2⅞"	5¾"	5½"		5½"	2¾"	2	28	4	24
6"	3⅜+	6⅞+	6½"		6½"	3¼"	2	24	4	20

\+ For finished dimensions followed by a "+," add 1/16" to the listed number.

TRUE OCTAGONS

The true octagon has eight equal sides and 135° angles. The proportions differ from the 9-Patch based Snowball on pages 58–59. You can choose from two cutting methods, depending on the tools you have on hand. If you want to use just a regular ruler, use the chart on this page. True octagons to fit other patches can be rotary cut in only Magic Measures sizes.

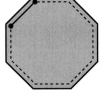 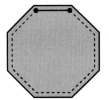 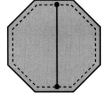

A. finished side   **A.** finished side   **B.** finished height 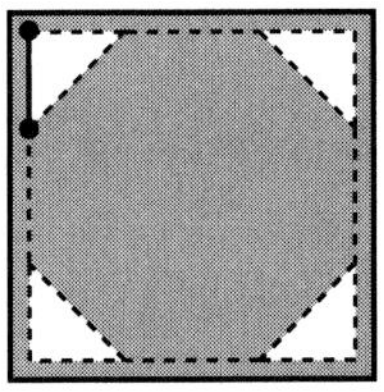   **C.** fits finished triangle

CUTTING DIRECTIONS

D. Find your chosen size listed in the Description columns of the chart below. Follow the line listing your octagon size to the right to Column D, the strip width. Cut a strip in the listed width, either 18" or 44" long.

D. Cut strip width.

E. Trim a sliver off the short end of the strip at a right angle to the long sides. (Trim the left end for right handers; the right end for left handers.) Parallel subcut (page 14) a square in the size listed in Column E.

E. Subcut a square.   straight grain

F. Lay the measurement listed in Column F over two opposite corners of the square. Cut parallel to the diagonal (page 16) along the ruler's edge. Keep the parts in a square. Repeat for the other diagonal.

G. Cut parallel to the newly cut side at the measurement listed in Column G. Repeat for the remaining side to complete an octagon.

Continue cutting octagons as shown in Figure G2.

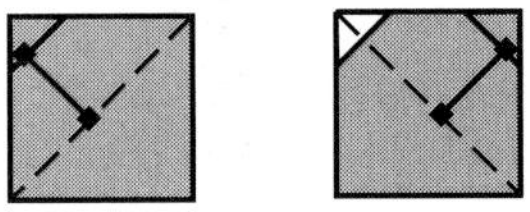

F. Cut parallel to the diagonal on 2 adjacent sides.   **G. Cut parallel to angled sides to complete octagon.**

G2. Continue cutting this way.

#M2: TRUE OCTAGONS

Description			Cutting Dimensions				Yield (Yardage)			
							18" strips		**44" strips**	
A. fin. side	B. fin. octagon height	C. fits fin. triangle	D. cut strip width	E. cut square	F. cut dist. from diag.	G. cut dist. from side	# per strip	# per yard	# per strip	# per yard
1¼"	3"	⅞"	3½"	3½"	1¾"	3½"	5	110	11	110
1½"	3⅝"	1+	4⅛"	4⅛"	2+	4⅛"	4	72	9	72
1¾"	4¼"	1¼"	4¾"	4¾"	2⅜"	4¾"	3	48	8	56
2⅛"	5⅛"	1½"	5⅝"	5⅝"	2¾+	5⅝"	3	42	7	42
2½"	6"	1¾"	6½"	6½"	3¼"	6½"	2	24	6	30
3"	7¼"	2⅛"	7¾"	7¾"	3⅞"	7¾"	2	20	5	20
3½"	8½"	2½"	9"	9"	4½"	9"	1	8	4	12
4¼"	10¼"	3"	10¾"	10¾"	5⅜"	10¾"	1	6	3	9

+ Cutting dimensions followed by "+" can be cut in the size listed using the black edge of the Rotaruler 16. If you prefer an ordinary rotary ruler, cut halfway between the listed number and the next larger one-eighth inch.

TRUE OCTAGONS USING S45

This is the same true octagon as the one on the facing page, but it is cut using an easier method. You will need a Shapemaker 45 tool to cut this way.

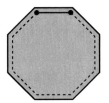

A. finished side

A. finished side

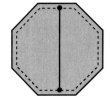

B. finished height

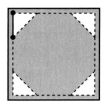

C. fits finished triangle

CUTTING DIRECTIONS

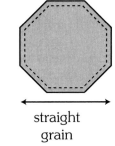

D. Find your chosen octagon listed in the Description columns of the chart below. Follow the line listing your octagon size to the right to Column D, the strip width. Cut a strip in the listed width, either 18" or 44" long.

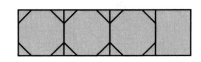

D. Cut strip width.

E. Trim a sliver off the short end of the strip at a right angle to the long sides. (Trim the left end for right handers; the right end for left handers.) Parallel subcut (page 14) a square in the size listed in Column E.

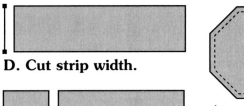

E. Subcut a square.

straight grain

F. Lay the Shapemaker 45 tool over the corner of the square, with the tool's long side aligned with one side and the measurement listed in Column F aligned with the adjacent side. See page 15. Make an S45 subcut to cut off a triangle. Repeat for the remaining three corners to complete an octagon.

Continue cutting octagons as shown in Figure F2.

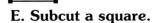

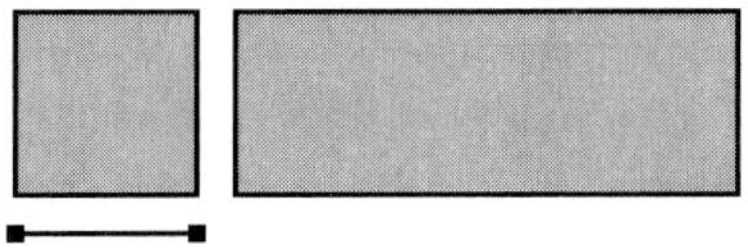

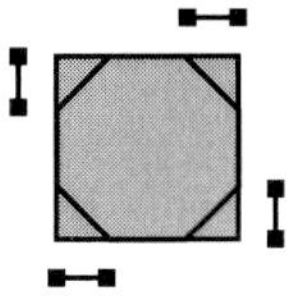

F. Cut off 4 triangles using S45.

F2. Continue cutting this way.

#M3: TRUE OCTAGONS USING SHAPEMAKER 45

Description			Cutting Dimensions			Yield (Yardage)			
						18" strips		44" strips	
A. fin. side	B. fin. octagon height	C. fits fin. triangle	D. cut strip width	E. cut square	F. cut off triangle	# per strip	# per yard	# per strip	# per yard
1¼"	3"	⅞"	3½"	3½"	1"	5	110	11	110
1¾"	4¼"	1¼"	4¾"	4¾"	1⅜"	3	48	8	56
2⅛"	5⅛"	1½"	5⅝"	5⅝"	1⅝"	3	42	7	42
2½"	6"	1¾"	6½"	6½"	1⅞"	2	24	6	30
3"	7¼"	2⅛"	7¾"	7¾"	2¼"	2	20	5	20
3½"	8½"	2½"	9"	9"	2⅝"	1	8	4	12
4¼"	10¼"	3"	10¾"	10¾"	3⅛"	1	6	3	9

+ For finished dimensions followed by a "+," add 1⁄16" to the listed number.

SNOWBALLS USING S45

The Snowball has four short and four longer sides. It fits a triangle having the same finished short and long sides. It is proportioned like a 9-Patch. You can choose from two cutting methods, depending on the tools you have on hand. The easier method is on this page. You will need a Shapemaker 45 tool to cut this way.

CUTTING DIRECTIONS

D. Find your chosen size listed in the Description columns of the chart below. Follow the line listing your Snowball size to the right to Column D, the strip width. Cut a strip in the listed width, either 18" or 44" long.

E. Trim a sliver off the short end of the strip at right angles to the long sides. (Trim the left end for right handers; the right end for left handers.) Parallel subcut (page 14) a square in the size listed in Column E.

F. Lay the Shapemaker 45 tool over the corner of the square, with the tool's long side aligned with one side and the measurement listed in Column F aligned with the adjacent side. See page 15. Make an S45 subcut to cut off a triangle. Repeat for the remaining three corners to complete a Snowball.

Continue cutting Snowballs as shown in Figure F2.

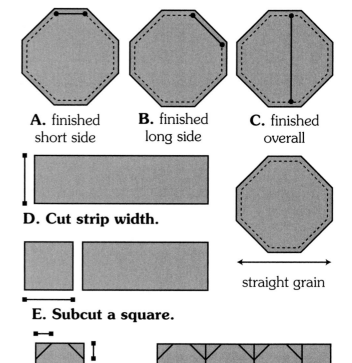

A. finished short side

B. finished long side

C. finished overall

D. Cut strip width.

straight grain

E. Subcut a square.

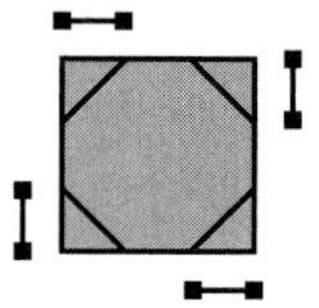

F. Cut off 4 triangles using S45.

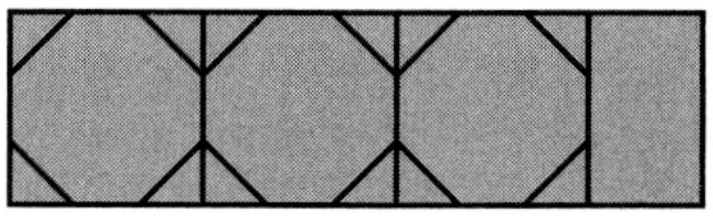

F2. Continue cutting this way.

#M4: SNOWBALLS USING SHAPEMAKER 45

Description			Cutting Dimensions			Yield (Yardage)			
						18" strips		44" strips	
A. fin. short side	B. fin. long side	C. fin. overall square	D. cut strip width	E. cut square	F. cut off triangle	# per strip	# per yard	# per strip	# per yard
⅞"	1¼"	2⅝"	3⅛"	3⅛"	1"	5	120	12	132
1"	1⅜+	3"	3½"	3½"	1⅛"	5	110	11	110
1¼"	1¾"	3¾"	4¼"	4¼"	1⅜"	4	72	9	72
1½"	2⅛"	4½"	5"	5"	1⅝"	3	48	8	56
1¾"	2½"	5¼"	5¾"	5¾"	1⅞"	3	36	6	36
2"	2¾+	6"	6½"	6½"	2⅛"	2	24	6	30
2⅛"	3"	6⅜"	6⅞"	6⅞"	2¼"	2	20	5	25
2½"	3½"	7½"	8"	8"	2⅝"	2	20	5	20
3"	4¼"	9"	9½"	9½"	3⅛"	1	8	4	12
3½"	4⅞+	10½"	11"	11"	3⅝"	1	6	3	9
3⅝"	5⅛"	10⅞"	11⅜"	11⅜"	3¾"	1	6	3	9
4"	5⅝+	12"	12½"	12½"	4⅛"	1	6	3	6

+ For finished dimensions followed by a "+," add ¹⁄₁₆" to the listed number.

MORE SNOWBALLS

This is the same Snowball as the one on the facing page, but it is cut with a different method. If you want to use just a regular ruler, use the chart on this page.

D. Cut strip width.

CUTTING DIRECTIONS

D. Find your chosen size listed in the Description columns of the chart below. Follow the line listing your Snowball size to the right to Column D, the strip width. Cut a strip in the listed width, either 18" or 44" long.

E. Trim a sliver off the short end of the strip at right angles to the long sides. (Trim the left end for right handers; the right end for left handers.) Parallel subcut (page 14) a square in the size listed in Column E.

F. Lay the measurement listed in Column F over two opposite corners of the square. Cut parallel to the diagonal (page 16) along the ruler's edge. Keep the square parts in position. Repeat for the other diagonal.

G. Cut parallel to the newly cut side at the measurement listed in Column G. Repeat for the remaining side to complete a Snowball.

Continue cutting Snowballs as shown in Figure G2.

E. Subcut a square.

F. Cut parallel to the diagonal on 2 adjacent sides.

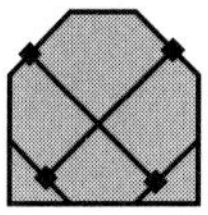

G. Cut parallel to angled sides to make a Snowball.

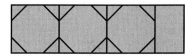

G2. Continue cutting this way.

#M5: SNOWBALLS (UNEVEN OCTAGONS)

Description			Cutting Dimensions				Yield (Yardage)			
							18" strips		44" strips	
A. fin. short side	B. fin. long side	C. fin. over-all square	D. cut strip width	E. cut square	F. cut dist. from diag.	G. cut dist. from side	# per strip	# per yard	# per strip	# per yard
⅞"	1¼"	2⅝"	3⅛"	3⅛"	1½"	3"	5	120	12	132
1+	1½"	3⅛+	3⅝+	3⅝+	1¾"	3½"	4	80	10	90
1¼"	1¾"	3¾"	4¼"	4¼"	2"	4"	4	72	9	72
1⅜+	2"	4¼"	4¾"	4¾"	2¼"	4½"	3	48	8	56
1½"	2⅛"	4½"	5"	5"	2⅜"	4¾"	3	48	8	56
1¾"	2½"	5¼"	5¾"	5¾"	2¾"	5½"	3	36	6	36
2"	2¾+	6"	6½"	6½"	3+	6⅛"	2	24	6	30
2⅛"	3"	6⅜"	6⅞"	6⅞"	3¼"	6½"	2	20	5	25
2½"	3½"	7½"	8"	8"	3¾"	7½"	2	20	5	20
2¾+	4"	8½"	9"	9"	4¼"	8½"	1	8	4	12
3"	4¼"	9"	9½"	9½"	4½"	9"	1	8	4	12

+   For finished dimensions followed by a "+," add ¹⁄₁₆" to the listed number.

BOW TIES

The Bow Tie shape is a square with a triangle clipped off one corner. The finished short side of the triangle is half the finished side of the square. You can choose from two cutting methods, depending on the tools you have on hand. If you want to use just a regular ruler, use the chart on this page. If you have an S45, see page 61.

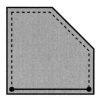
A. finished long side

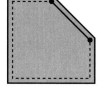
B. finished med. side

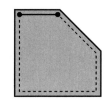
C. finished short side

CUTTING DIRECTIONS

D. Find your chosen size listed in the Description columns of the chart below. Follow the line listing your Bow Tie size to the right to Column D, the strip width. Cut a strip in the listed width, either 18" or 44" long.

E. Trim a sliver off the short end of the strip at right angles to the long sides. (Trim the left end for right handers; the right end for left handers.) Parallel subcut (page 14) a square in the size listed in Column E.

F. Lay the measurement listed in Column F over two opposite corners of the square. Cut parallel to the diagonal (page 16) along the ruler's edge. This completes a Bow Tie.
    Continue cutting Bow Ties as shown in Figure F2.

D. Cut strip width.

straight grain

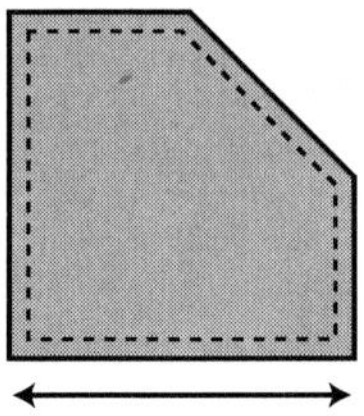

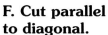
E. Subcut a square.

F. Cut parallel to diagonal. **F2. Continue cutting this way.**

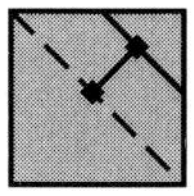

#M6: BOW TIES

Description			Cutting			Yield (Yardage)			
						18" strips		44" strips	
A. fin. long side	B. fin. med. side	C. fin. short side	D. cut strip width	E. cut square	F. cut dist. from diag.	# per strip	# per yard	# per strip	# per yard
1¾"	1¼"	⅞"	2¼"	2¼"	⅞"	7	238	17	255
2⅛"	1½"	1+	2⅝"	2⅝"	1"	6	180	15	195
2½"	1¾"	1¼"	3"	3"	1⅛"	5	130	13	143
3"	2⅛"	1½"	3½"	3½"	1¼+	5	110	11	110
3½"	2½"	1¾"	4"	4"	1½"	4	80	10	80
4"	2¾+	2"	4½"	4½"	1⅝+	3	48	8	56
4¼"	3"	2⅛"	4¾"	4¾"	1¾"	3	48	8	56
5"	3½"	2½"	5½"	5½"	2"	3	42	7	42
6"	4¼"	3"	6½"	6½"	2⅜"	2	24	6	30

+ Cutting dimensions followed by "+" can be cut in the size listed using the black edge of the Rotaruler 16. If you prefer an ordinary rotary ruler, cut halfway between the listed number and the next larger one-eighth inch.

MORE BOW TIES

The Bow Tie shape is a square with a triangle clipped off one corner. The finished short side of the triangle is half the finished side of the square. You can choose from two cutting methods, depending on the tools you have on hand. If you have an S45, use this chart. If you want to use just a regular ruler, use the chart on page 60.

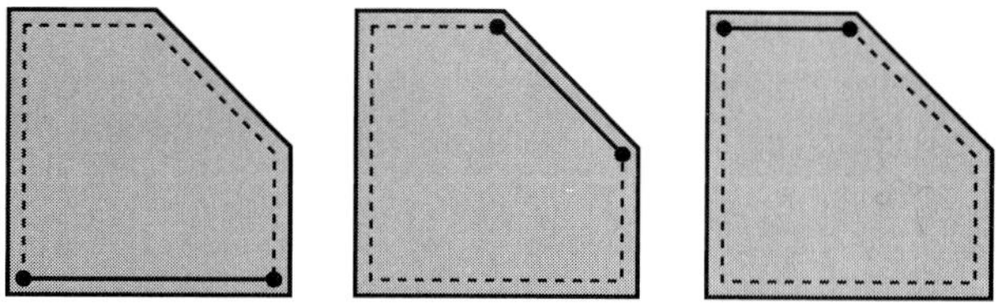

A. finished long side

B. finished med. side

C. finished short side

CUTTING DIRECTIONS

D. Find your chosen size listed in the Description columns of the chart below. Follow the line listing your Bow Tie size to the right to Column D, the strip width. Cut a strip in the listed width, either 18" or 44" long.

E. Trim a sliver off the short end of the strip at a right angle to the long sides. (Trim the left end for right handers; the right end for left handers.) Parallel subcut (page 14) a square in the size listed in Column E.

F. See S45 subcutting on page 15. Lay the Shapemaker 45 tool over the corner of the square, with the tool's long side aligned with one side and the measurement listed in Column F aligned with the adjacent side. Cut off a triangle. This completes a Bow Tie.

Continue cutting Bow Ties as shown in Figure F2.

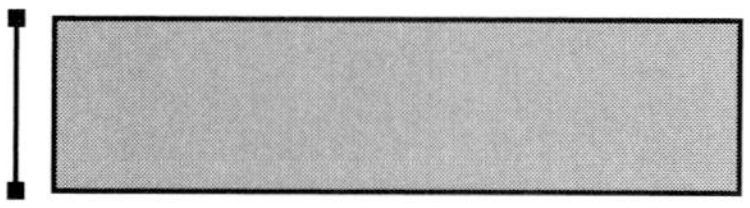

D. Cut strip width.

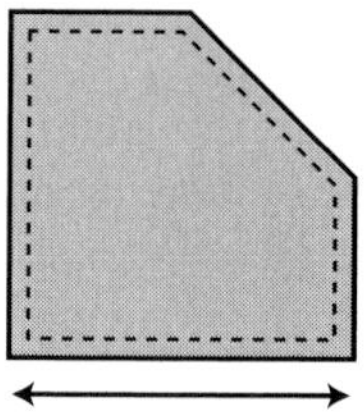

straight grain

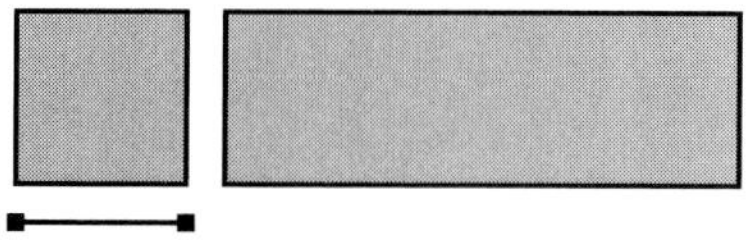

E. Subcut a square.

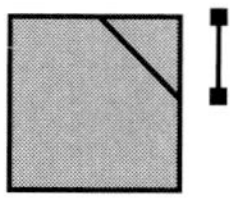

F. Cut off a triangle using the S45.

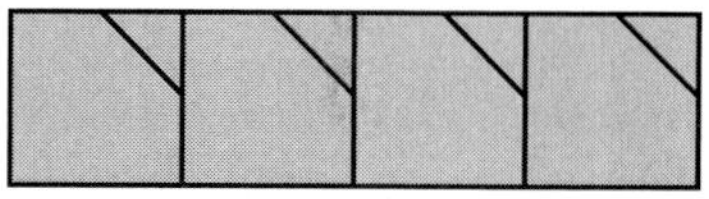

F2. Continue cutting this way.

#M7: BOW TIES USING SHAPEMAKER 45

Description			Cutting			Yield (Yardage)			
						18" strips		44" strips	
A. fin. long side	B. fin. med. side	C. fin. short side	D. cut strip width	E. cut square	F. cut off triangle	# per strip	# per yard	# per strip	# per yard
1¾"	1¼"	⅞"	2¼"	2¼"	1"	7	238	17	255
2"	1⅜+	1"	2½"	2½"	1⅛"	7	224	16	224
2½"	1¾"	1¼"	3"	3"	1⅜"	5	130	13	143
3"	2⅛"	1½"	3½"	3½"	1⅝"	5	110	11	110
3½"	2½"	1¾"	4"	4"	1⅞"	4	80	10	80
4"	2¾+	2"	4½"	4½"	2⅛"	3	48	8	56
4¼"	3"	2⅛"	4¾"	4¾"	2¼"	3	48	8	56
5"	3½"	2½"	5½"	5½"	2⅝"	3	42	7	42
6"	4¼"	3"	6½"	6½"	3⅛"	2	24	6	30

+ For finished dimensions followed by a "+," add 1/16" to the listed number.

90° KITES

The finished 90° kite's short side equals half its height and width. This is the kite found in Skyrocket and Sweethearts' Star Blocks. It is often used with the triangles on pages 48–49.

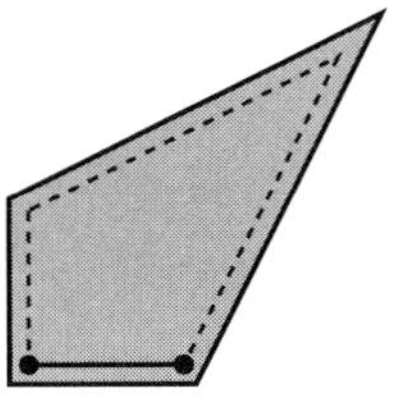

A. finished short side

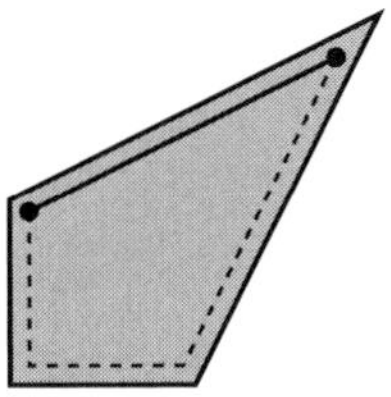

B. finished long side

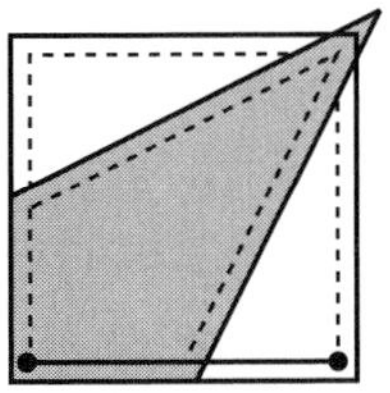

C. fits finished square

CUTTING DIRECTIONS

D. Find your chosen size listed in the Description columns of the chart below. Follow the line listing your kite size to the right to Column D, the strip width. Cut a strip in the listed width, either 18" or 44" long.

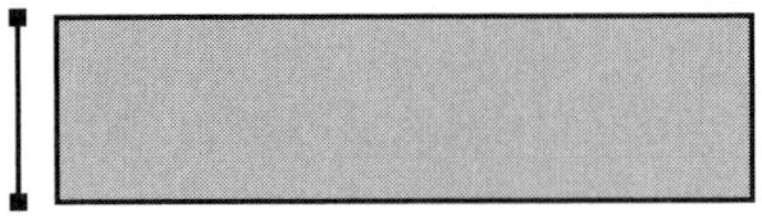

D. Cut strip width.

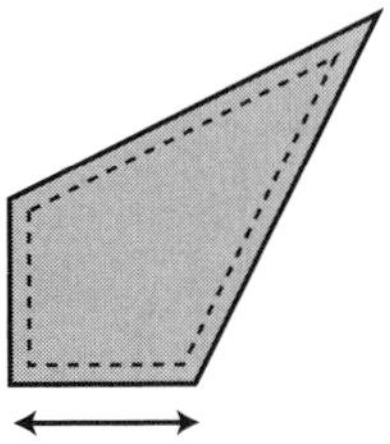

straight grain

E. Trim a sliver off the short end of the strip at a right angle to the long sides. (Trim the left end for right handers; the right end for left handers.) Parallel subcut (page 14) a square in the size listed in Column E.

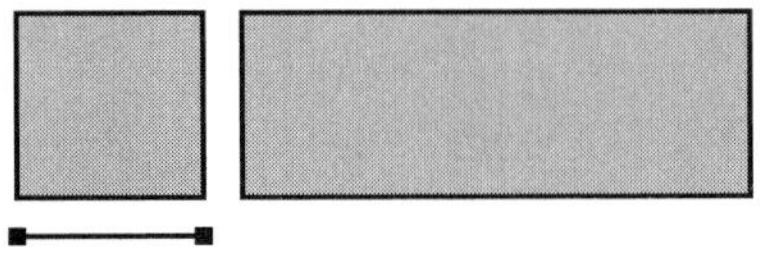

E. Subcut a square.

F. See page 16 for detailed figures and instructions for cutting 2:1 angles. Lay a gridded ruler over the fabric square, with one corner of the ruler's grid at the corner of the fabric. Keeping the corner in position, tilt the ruler so that the fabric edge makes a diagonal across 2:1 rectangles of the ruler's grid. (The 2:1 rectangles comprise 2 adjacent grid squares.) Cut along the edge of the ruler to remove a triangular piece. Repeat from the same corner to cut a second triangle off the adjacent side to complete the kite.

Continue cutting kites as shown in Figure F2.

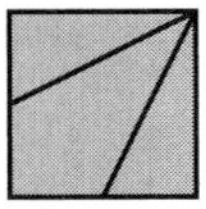

F. Cut off 2 corners at 2:1 angles.

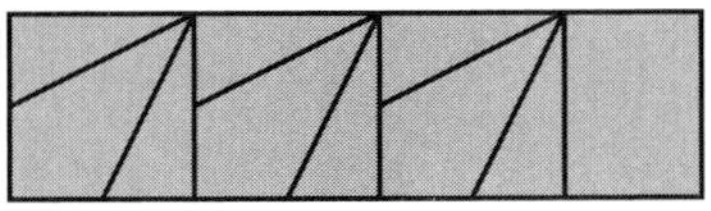

F2. Continue cutting this way.

#M8: RIGHT ANGLE KITES

Description			Cutting			Yield (Yardage)			
						18" strips		44" strips	
A. fin. short side	B. fin. long side	C. fits fin. square	D. cut strip width	E. cut square	F.	# per strip	# per yard	# per strip	# per yard
⅞"	1⅞+	1¾"	2½+	2½+	cut off two corners at 2:1 angle	6	180	15	195
1"	2¼"	2"	2¾+	2¾+		6	168	14	168
1+	2⅜"	2⅛"	2⅞+	2⅞+		5	130	13	143
1¼"	2¾+	2½"	3¼+	3¼+		5	120	12	120
1½"	3⅜"	3"	3¾+	3¾+		4	80	10	90
1¾"	3⅞+	3½"	4¼+	4¼+		4	72	9	72
2"	4½"	4"	4¾+	4¾+		3	48	8	56
2⅛"	4¾"	4¼"	5+	5+		3	42	7	42
2½"	5½+	5"	5¾+	5¾+		3	36	6	36
3"	6⅝+	6"	6¾+	6¾+		2	20	5	25

\+ Cutting dimensions followed by "+" can be cut in the size listed using the black edge of the Rotaruler 16. If you prefer an ordinary rotary ruler, cut halfway between the listed number and the next larger one-eighth inch.

135° KITES

This 135° kite is made from an isosceles right triangle with a smaller triangle cut off. Its two long sides are equal. This kite is found in true eight-pointed stars. The chart below lists only the sizes that allow you to also rotary cut the small triangles to fit it. (The finished short side is the same for the small triangle and kite.)

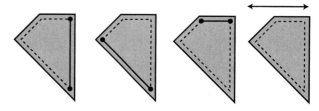

A. finished long side   **A.** finished long side   **B.** finished short side   straight grain

CUTTING DIRECTIONS

C. Find your chosen size listed in the Description columns of the chart below. Follow the line listing your kite size to the right to Column C, the strip width. Cut a strip in the listed width, either 18" or 44" long.

C. Cut strip width.

D. Trim a sliver off the short end of the strip at a right angle to the long sides. (Trim the left end for right handers; the right end for left handers.) Parallel subcut (page 14) a square in the size listed in Column D.

D. Subcut a square.

E. Cut in half diagonally.

E. Cut the square in half diagonally (page 15), laying the ruler's edge from corner to opposite corner of the square.

F. See page 15 for details of right angle subcutting. Align the ruling listed in Column F with the point of the triangle. Align any line that crosses the listed ruling with the long edge of the triangle. Cut along the ruler's edge, which is at a right angle to the triangle's long side, to complete a kite.

Continue cutting kites as shown in Figure F2.

F. Cut at right angle to long side.

F2. Continue cutting this way.

#M9: 135° KITES

Description		Cutting				Yield (Yardage)			
A. fin. long side	**B. fin. short side**	**C. cut strip width**	**D. cut square**	**E.** cut in half diagonally into 2 triangles	**F. cut long side**	**18" strips**		**44" strips**	
						# per strip	**# per yard**	**# per strip**	**# per yard**
1½"	⅝"	2⅜"	2⅜"		2⅜"	14	448	32	448
1¾"	¾"	2⅝"	2⅝"		2⅝"	12	360	30	390
2⅛"	⅞"	3"	3"		3"	10	260	26	286
2½"	1"	3⅜"	3⅜"		3⅜"	10	220	22	220
3"	1¼"	3⅞"	3⅞"		3⅞"	8	160	20	180
3⅛+	1¼+	4+	4+		4+	8	144	18	144
3½"	1⅜+	4⅜"	4⅜"		4⅜"	8	144	18	144
3⅝"	1½"	4½"	4½"		4½"	6	96	16	112
4¼"	1¾"	5⅛"	5⅛"		5⅛"	6	84	14	84
4½"	1⅞"	5⅜"	5⅜"		5⅜"	6	84	14	84
5⅛"	2⅛"	6"	6"		6"	4	48	12	60
6"	2½"	6⅞"	6⅞"		6⅞"	4	40	10	50

+ See note below chart on facing page.

DIAGONAL TRAPEZOIDS

The trapezoids in this chart are usually tilted in the block. This puts the straight grain along the edge of the block or unit. This finished trapezoid is proportioned so that the distance between parallel sides is half the medium side and the medium side is half the long side.

CUTTING DIRECTIONS

D. Find your chosen size listed in the Description columns of the chart below. You may identify the trapezoid based on any of its sides. Follow the line listing your trapezoid size to the right for cutting directions and yield. Find the strip width in Column D of the Cutting box. Cut a strip in the listed width, either 18" or 44" long.

E. Trim a sliver off the left end of the strip at a right angle to the long sides. (Trim the right end for left handers.) Make a parallel subcut (page 14) of the size listed in Column E to complete a square.

F. Cut the square in half diagonally (page 15) to make two triangles as shown.

G. Make a subcut parallel to the long side of the triangle (page 14) at the distance listed in Column G to make one trapezoid from each triangle.

Continue cutting trapezoids as shown in Figure G2.

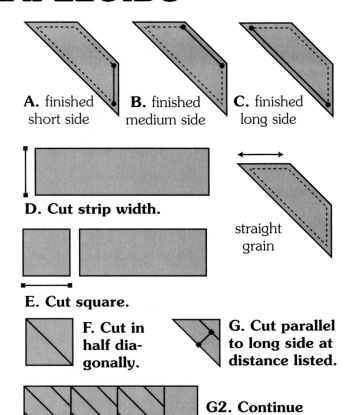

A. finished short side **B.** finished medium side **C.** finished long side

D. Cut strip width.

straight grain

E. Cut square.

F. Cut in half diagonally.

G. Cut parallel to long side at distance listed.

G2. Continue cutting this way.

#Z1: DIAGONAL TRAPEZOIDS

Description			Cutting				Yield (Yardage)			
							18" strips		44" strips	
A. fin. short side	B. fin. med. side	C. fin. long side	D. cut strip width	E. cut square	F. cut diagonally into 2 triangles	G. cut dist. from side	# per strip	# per yard	# per strip	# per yard
⅞"	1¼"	2½"	2⅝"	2⅝"		1⅛"	12	360	30	390
1+	1½"	3"	3"	3"		1¼"	10	260	26	286
1¼"	1¾"	3½"	3⅜"	3⅜"		1⅜"	10	220	22	220
1⅜+	2"	4"	3⅝+	3⅝+		1½"	8	160	20	180
1½"	2⅛"	4¼"	3⅞"	3⅞"		1½+	8	160	20	180
1¾"	2½"	5"	4⅜"	4⅜"		1¾"	8	144	18	144
2"	2¾+	5⅝+	4⅞"	4⅞"		1⅞+	6	96	16	112
2⅛"	3"	6"	5⅛"	5⅛"		2"	6	84	14	84
2½"	3½"	7"	5⅞"	5⅞"		2¼"	4	48	12	60
2¾+	4"	8"	6½"	6½"		2½"	4	48	12	60
3"	4¼"	8½"	6⅞"	6⅞"		2⅝"	4	40	10	50

+ Cutting dimensions followed by "+" can be cut in the size listed using the black edge of the Rotaruler 16. If you prefer an ordinary rotary ruler, cut halfway between the listed number and the next larger one-eighth inch.

MORE DIAGONAL TRAPEZOIDS

The only difference between the trapezoids in this chart and those in the previous chart is in the cutting method for one step. The trapezoids below are cut using the Shapemaker 45 tool for Step G. The finished trapezoid is proportioned like the one on page 64.

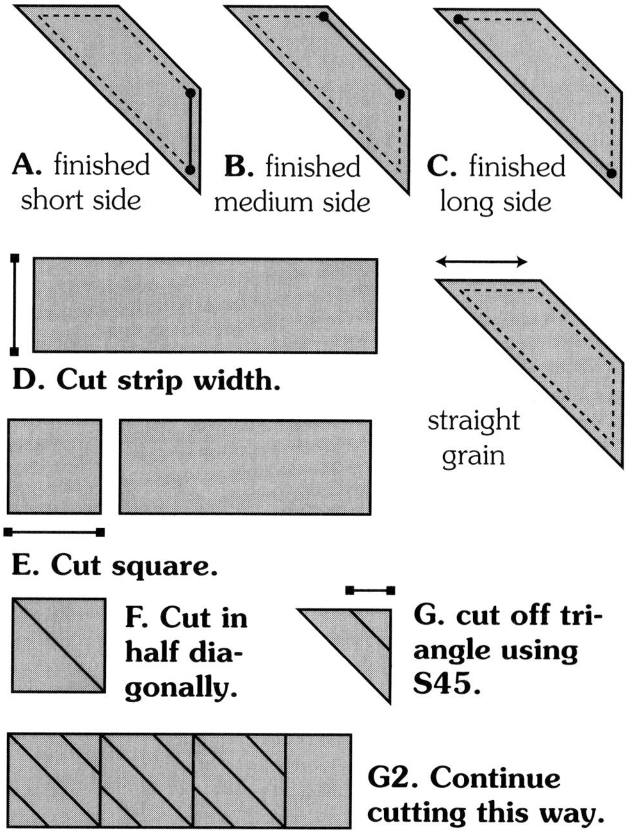

A. finished short side
B. finished medium side
C. finished long side
D. Cut strip width.
straight grain
E. Cut square.
F. Cut in half diagonally.
G. cut off triangle using S45.
G2. Continue cutting this way.

CUTTING DIRECTIONS

D. Find your chosen size listed in the Description columns of the chart below. You may identify the trapezoid based on any of its sides. Follow the line listing your trapezoid size to the right for cutting directions and yield. Find the strip width in Column D of the Cutting box. Cut a strip in the listed width, either 18" or 44" long.

E. Trim a sliver off the short end of the strip at a right angle to the long sides. Make a parallel subcut (page 14) of the size listed in Column E to complete a square.

F. Cut the square in half diagonally (page 15) to make two triangles as shown.

G. S45 subcut (page 15) a triangle of the size listed in Column G, measuring from the 90° corner and cutting along the angled short side of the S45 tool. Make one trapezoid from each of the two triangles.

Continue cutting trapezoids as shown in Figure G2.

#Z2: DIAGONAL TRAPEZOIDS USING SHAPEMAKER 45

Description			Cutting				Yield (Yardage)			
							18" strips		44" strips	
A. fin. short side	B. fin. med. side	C. fin. long side	D. cut strip width	E. cut square	F. cut in half diagonally	G. cut off triangle	# per strip	# per yard	# per strip	# per yard
⅞"	1¼"	2½"	2⅝"	2⅝"		1"	12	360	30	390
1"	1⅜+	2¾+	2⅞"	2⅞"		1⅛"	12	312	26	312
1+	1½"	3"	3"	3"		1⅛+	10	260	26	286
1¼"	1¾"	3½"	3⅜"	3⅜"		1⅜"	10	220	22	220
1½"	2⅛"	4¼"	3⅞"	3⅞"		1⅝"	8	160	20	180
1¾"	2½"	5"	4⅜"	4⅜"		1⅞"	8	144	18	144
2"	2¾+	5⅝+	4⅞"	4⅞"		2⅛"	6	96	16	112
2⅛"	3"	6"	5⅛"	5⅛"		2¼"	6	84	14	84
2½"	3½"	7"	5⅞"	5⅞"		2⅝"	4	48	12	60
3"	4¼"	8½"	6⅞"	6⅞"		3⅛"	4	40	10	50

+ Cutting dimensions followed by "+" can be cut in the size listed using the black edge of the Rotaruler 16. If you prefer an ordinary rotary ruler, cut halfway between the listed number and the next larger one-eighth inch.

TRAPEZOIDS

The trapezoids in this chart are proportioned with the width equal to the short side and the long side three times the short side. For trapezoids of other proportions (and having 45° angles), cut the strip the finished width plus ½" and cut the trapezoid length the finished long side plus 1¼".

If you don't have an S45, use the strip width (D) and trapezoid length (F) dimensions listed to cut rectangles. Then cut off the two short ends at a 45° angle from two adjacent corners. Trapezoids cut from rectangles waste fabric, and the yields listed no longer apply.

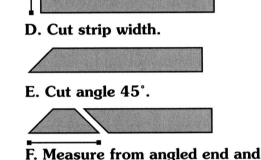

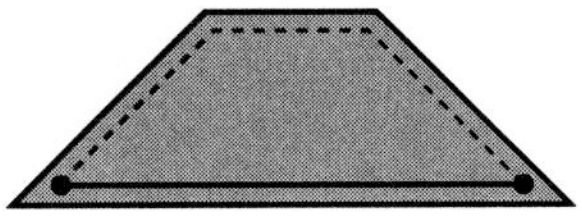

A. finished long side 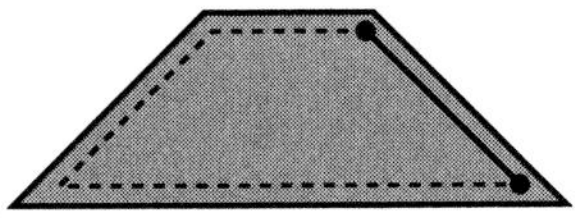 **B.** finished angled side

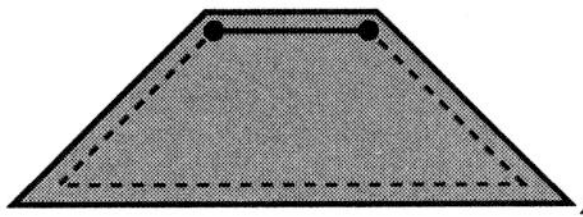

C. finished short side ⟷ straight grain

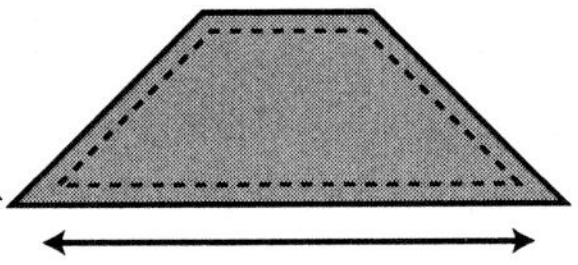

CUTTING DIRECTIONS

D. Find your chosen size listed in the Description columns of the chart below. You may identify the trapezoid based on any of its sides. Follow the line listing your trapezoid size to the right for cutting directions and yield. Find the strip width in Column D of the Cutting box. Cut a strip in the listed width, either 18" or 44" long. (Do *not* use the S45 for this cut.)

E. Cut off the upper left corner at a 45° angle.

F. Make an S45 subcut (page 15) using the Shapemaker 45 tool. Lay the ruling listed in Column F over the point of the strip. Lay the base (long side) of the tool along the long side of the strip. Cut along the angled short side of the ruler.

Continue cutting trapezoids as shown in Figure F2, turning the ruler after each cut.

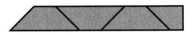

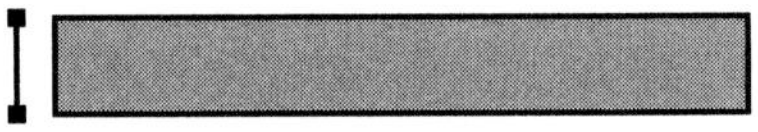

D. Cut strip width.

E. Cut angle 45°.

F. Measure from angled end and cut trapezoid using S45.

F2. Continue cutting this way.

#Z3: TRAPEZOIDS USING SHAPEMAKER 45

Description			Cutting			Yield (Yardage)			
						18" strips		44" strips	
A. fin long side	B. fin angled side	C. fin short side	D. cut strip width	E. cut angle 45°	F. cut trapezoid length	# per strip	# per yard	# per strip	# per yard
2⅝"	1¼"	⅞"	1⅜"		3⅞"	6	348	15	375
3"	1⅜+	1"	1½"		4¼"	5	260	14	322
3¾"	1¾"	1¼"	1¾"		5"	4	176	11	220
4½"	2⅛"	1½"	2"		5¾"	4	160	10	170
5¼"	2½"	1¾"	2¼"		6½"	3	102	8	120
6"	2¾+	2"	2½"		7¼"	3	96	7	98
6⅜"	3"	2⅛"	2⅝"		7⅝"	2	60	7	91
7½"	3½"	2½"	3"		8¾"	2	52	6	66

+ For finished dimensions followed by a "+," add ¹⁄₁₆" to the listed number.

HALF TRAPEZOIDS

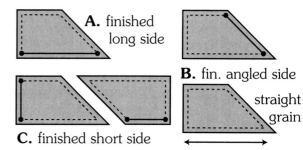

These half trapezoids are proportioned with equal width and short side. The long side is double the width.

The Shapemaker 45 is the best tool for Step E. If you don't have an S45, cut strips as listed. Then cut rectangles using the half trapezoid (E) dimension listed. Finally, cut off one short end at a 45° angle from the corner. Cutting a single half trapezoid from a rectangle wastes fabric, and the yields listed no longer apply.

A. finished long side

B. fin. angled side — straight grain

C. finished short side

CUTTING DIRECTIONS

D. Find your chosen size listed in the Description columns of the chart below. Follow the line listing your trapezoid size to the right for cutting directions. Cut a strip in the width listed in Column D, either 18" or 44" long.

D. Cut strip width.

E. Trim a sliver off the end of the strip at right angles to the long sides. Make an S45 subcut (page 15) as follows. Lay the base of the S45 tool over the long side of the strip. Align the ruling listed in Column E with the strip's end. Cut along the short side of the S45 to make a half trapezoid.

E. Use the S45 to sub-cut a half trapezoid.

F. Use a regular ruler to make a right angle subcut (page 15) to cut another half trapezoid from the strip. Align the listed ruling with the point of the strip. Align any ruling that crosses the first one with the long edge of the strip. Cut parallel to the listed ruling along the edge of your ruler.

F. Right angle subcut a half trapezoid.

Continue cutting half trapezoids, alternating E and F steps as shown.

F2. Continue this way.

#Z4: HALF TRAPEZOIDS USING SHAPEMAKER 45

Description			Cutting Dimensions			Yield (Yardage)			
						18" strips		44" strips	
A. fin. long side	B. fin. angled side	C. fin. short side	D. cut strip width	E. cut half trapezoid	F. cut half trapezoid	# per strip	# per yard	# per strip	# per yard
1¾"	1¼"	⅞"	1⅜"	2⅝"	2⅝"	8	464	20	500
2"	1⅜+	1"	1½"	2⅞"	2⅞"	8	416	18	414
2⅛"	1½"	1+	1½+	3"	3"	7	350	18	396
2½"	1¾"	1¼"	1¾"	3⅜"	3⅜"	6	264	16	320
3"	2⅛"	1½"	2"	3⅞"	3⅞"	6	240	13	221
3½"	2½"	1¾"	2¼"	4⅜"	4⅜"	5	170	12	180
4"	2¾+	2"	2½"	4⅞"	4⅞"	4	128	10	140
4¼"	3"	2⅛"	2⅝"	5⅛"	5⅛"	4	120	10	130
5"	3½"	2½"	3"	5⅞"	5⅞"	4	104	8	88
6"	4¼"	3"	3½"	6⅞"	6⅞"	3	66	7	70
7"	4⅞+	3½"	4"	7⅞"	7⅞"	2	40	6	48
7¼"	5⅛"	3⅝"	4⅛"	8⅛"	8⅛"	2	36	6	48
8"	5⅝+	4"	4½"	8⅞"	8⅞"	2	32	6	42

+ See notes below chart on page 65.

DIAGONAL HALF TRAPEZOIDS

The half trapezoids on these two pages are proportioned with equal width and short side. The long side is double the width. They are typically tilted in the block as shown here. This puts the straight grain around the edge of the block or unit.

The same shapes can be cut two ways, using different tools, as shown here and on the next page.

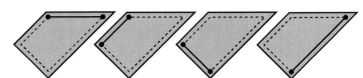

A. finished angled side   **B.** finished short side   **B.** finished short side   **C.** finished long side

CUTTING DIRECTIONS

D. Find your chosen size listed in the Description columns of the chart below. Follow the line listing your trapezoid size to the right for cutting directions. Use your regular ruler to cut a strip in the width listed in Column D, either 18" or 44" long.

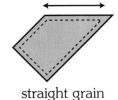

straight grain

D. Cut strip width.

E. Trim off the lower left corner of the strip at a 45° angle. (Left handers trim off the the lower right corner.)

E. Cut off end at 45° angle.

F. Use the Shapemaker 45 tool to S45 subcut (page 15) a triangle as follows. Lay the listed ruling over the point of the strip. Lay the base (long side) of the tool along the long edge of the strip. Cut along the angled edge of the S45 ruler to complete a triangle as shown.

F. S45 subcut the strip to make a triangle.

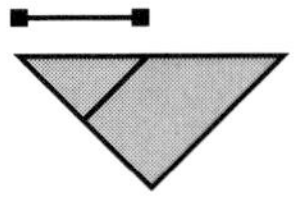

G. S45 subcut a triangle to complete a half trapezoid.

G. Once again make an S45 subcut (page 15) to cut off one point of the triangle to complete the half trapezoid. Lay the listed ruling over the point of the strip. Lay the base (long side) of the tool along the long edge of the triangle. Cut along the angled edge of the S45 to complete a half trapezoid as shown.

Continue cutting half trapezoids as shown in G2.

G2. Continue cutting this way.

#Z5: DIAGONAL HALF TRAPEZOIDS USING S45

Description			Cutting Dimensions				Yield (Yardage)			
A. fin. angled side	**B. fin. short side**	**C. fin. long side**	**D. cut strip width**	**E. cut angle 45°**	**F. cut triangle (S45)**	**G. cut off triangle**	18" strips		44" strips	
							# per strip	**# per yard**	**# per strip**	**# per yard**
1¼"	⅞"	1¾"	1⅞"		3¾"	1¾"	8	336	20	360
1¾"	1¼"	2½"	2⅜"		4¾"	2¼"	6	192	15	210
2⅛"	1½"	3"	2¾"		5½"	2⅝"	5	140	13	156
2½"	1¾"	3½"	3⅛"		6¼"	3"	4	96	11	121
3"	2⅛"	4¼"	3⅝"		7¼"	3½"	3	66	10	90
3½"	2½"	5"	4⅛"		8¼"	4"	3	54	8	64
4¼"	3"	6"	4⅞"		9¾"	4¾"	2	32	7	49

+   For finished dimensions followed by a "+," add 1/16" to the listed number.

MORE DIAGONAL HALF TRAPEZOIDS

This is the same diagonal half trapezoid as the one on the facing page. A different cutting method requiring just a regular ruler is used in this version.

D. Cut strip width.

CUTTING DIRECTIONS

D. Find your chosen size listed in the Description columns of the chart below. Follow the line listing your trapezoid size to the right for cutting directions. Cut a strip in the width listed in Column D, either 18" or 44" long.

E. Cut off end at 45° angle.

E. Trim off the end of the strip (lower left corner for right handers; lower right for left handers) at a 45° angle.

F. Make a subcut parallel to the angled end of the strip (page 14) to make a parallelogram.

F. Cut a parallelogram.

G. Cut the parallelogram in half diagonally.

G. Cut the parallelogram in half diagonally (page 15) to make two triangles.

H. Make a parallel subcut (page 14), measuring from the short side of the triangle, to complete the half trapezoid. Cut another half trapezoid from the second triangle.

Continue cutting half trapezoids from the strip as shown in Figure H2.

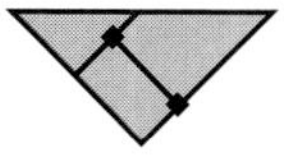

H. Parallel subcut as shown.

H2. Continue cutting this way.

#Z6: DIAGONAL HALF TRAPEZOIDS

Description			Cutting Dimensions					Yield (Yardage)			
								18" strips		44" strips	
A. fin. angled side	B. fin. short side	C. fin. long side	D. cut strip width	E. cut angle 45°	F. cut parallelogram	G. cut diagonally into 2 triangles	H. cut dist. from side	# per strip	# per yard	# per strip	# per yard
1¼"	⅞"	1¾"	1⅞"		2⅝"		1⅜"	8	336	20	360
1½"	1+	2⅛"	2⅛"		3"		1½+	7	252	17	272
1¾"	1¼"	2½"	2⅜"		3⅜"		1¾"	6	192	15	210
2"	1⅜+	2¾+	2⅝"		3⅝+		1⅞+	5	150	14	182
2⅛"	1½"	3"	2¾"		3⅞"		2"	5	140	13	156
2½"	1¾"	3½"	3⅛"		4⅜"		2¼"	4	96	11	121
2¾+	2"	4"	3⅜+		4⅞"		2½"	4	88	10	100
3"	2⅛"	4¼"	3⅝"		5⅛"		2⅝"	3	66	10	90
3½"	2½"	5"	4⅛"		5⅞"		3"	3	54	8	64
4"	2¾+	5⅝+	4⅝"		6½"		3¼+	2	32	7	49
4¼"	3"	6"	4⅞"		6⅞"		3½"	2	32	7	49

+ Cutting dimensions followed by "+" can be cut in the size listed using the black edge of the Rotaruler 16. If you prefer an ordinary rotary ruler, cut halfway between the listed number and the next larger one-eighth inch.

DIAMOND HALF TRAPEZOIDS

This half trapezoid is proportioned with two equal long sides. The short side plus the medium side equal the long side. It is proportioned like a diamond with a triangle cut off. This shape is often used with 45° diamonds (page 50).

A. finished long side   **A.** finished long side   **B.** finished medium side

The Shapemaker 45 is the best tool for Step E. If you don't have an S45, cut strips as listed. Then cut rectangles using the half trapezoid (E) dimensions listed. Finally, cut off one short end at a 45° angle from the corner. Cutting a single half trapezoid from a rectangle wastes fabric, and the yields listed no longer apply. Folded fabric results in mirror images.

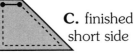

C. finished short side   straight grain

CUTTING DIRECTIONS

D. Cut strip width.

D. Find your chosen size listed in the Description columns of the chart below. Follow the line listing your trapezoid size to the right to Column D. Cut a strip in the width listed, either 18" or 44" long.

E. Use S45 to subcut a half trapezoid.

E. Trim a sliver off the end of the strip at a right angle to the long sides. (Trim the left end for right handers; the right end for left handers.) Make an S45 subcut (page 15) as follows. Lay the base of the S45 tool over the long side of the strip. Align the listed ruling with the end of the strip. Cut along the angled side of the S45 to make a half trapezoid.

F. Use regular ruler to right angle cut a half trapezoid.

F. Use a regular ruler to make a right angle subcut (page 15) to cut another half trapezoid from the strip. Align the listed ruling with the point of the strip. Align any ruling that crosses the first ruling with the long edge of the strip. Cut parallel to the listed ruling along the edge of your ruler to complete a half trapezoid.

Continue cutting half trapezoids, alternating steps E and F, as in F2.

F2. Continue cutting this way.

#Z7: DIAMOND HALF TRAPEZOIDS USING S45

Description			Cutting Dimensions			Yield (Yardage)			
						18" strips		44" strips	
A. fin. long side	B. fin. med. side	C. fin. short side	D. cut strip width	E. cut trape-zoid	F. cut trape-zoid	# per strip	# per yard	# per strip	# per yard
2⅛"	1½"	⅝"	2"	3"	3"	8	320	20	340
2½"	1¾"	¾"	2¼"	3⅜"	3⅜"	7	238	17	255
3"	2⅛"	⅞"	2⅝"	3⅞"	3⅞"	6	180	15	195
3½"	2½"	1"	3"	4⅜"	4⅜"	6	156	13	143
4¼"	3"	1¼"	3½"	5⅛"	5⅛"	4	88	11	110
4½"	3⅛+	1¼+	3⅝+	5⅜"	5⅜"	4	80	10	90
5⅛"	3⅝"	1½"	4⅛"	6"	6"	4	72	10	80
6"	4¼"	1¾"	4¾"	6⅞"	6⅞"	3	48	8	56

+ Cutting dimensions followed by "+" can be cut in the size listed using the black edge of the Rotaruler 16. If you prefer an ordinary rotary ruler, cut halfway between the listed number and the next larger one-eighth inch.

22½° HALF TRAPEZOIDS

These half trapezoids are proportioned like a 45°-22½°-112½° triangle with a similar triangle half its size cut off. It is useful for making many lovely four-pointed stars or eight-pointed stars. It is often paired with the triangle on page 44. Folded fabric yields mirror images.

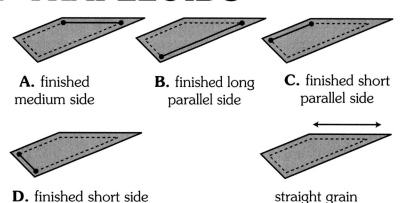

A. finished medium side

B. finished long parallel side

C. finished short parallel side

D. finished short side

straight grain

CUTTING DIRECTIONS

E. Find your chosen size listed in the Description columns of the chart below. Follow the line listing your trapezoid size to the right to Column E. This lists the appropriate finished long side of the triangle to be cut. Turn to page 44; find the matching number in Column A of the triangle chart; and cut a 45°-22½°-112½° triangle as described.

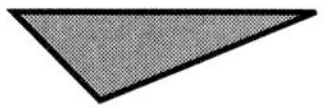

E. Cut a 45°-22½°-112½° triangle as shown on page 44.

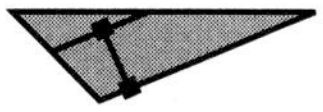

F. Subcut the triangle parallel to its medium side (page 14), using the measurement listed in Column F, below. Lay the listed ruling over the medium side of the triangle, and cut along the ruler's edge to complete a half trapezoid.

Continue cutting half trapezoids as shown.

F. Subcut the triangle parallel to the medium side.

F2. Continue cutting this way.

#Z8: 22½° HALF TRAPEZOIDS

Description				Cutting		Yield (Yardage)			
A. fin. med. side (str. grain)	B. fin. long parallel side	C. fin. short parallel side	D. fin. short side	E. cut triangle on p. 44: fin. long side	F. cut parallel to triangle's med. side	18" strips		44" strips	
						# per strip	# per yard	# per strip	# per yard
1"	1½"	¾"	⅜+	2"	⅞"	8	560	19	589
1¼"	1⅞+	⅞+	½"	2½"	1"	7	420	17	442
1½"	2¼+	1⅛"	⅝"	3"	1+	6	324	16	384
2"	3+	1½"	¾+	4"	1¼"	4	176	12	240
2⅛"	3¼"	1⅝"	⅞"	4¼"	1¼+	4	176	12	228
2¼"	3⅜+	1¾"	⅞+	4½"	1⅜"	4	168	11	198
2½"	3¾+	1⅞+	1+	5"	1⅜+	4	160	10	170
3"	4½+	2¼+	1¼"	6"	1⅝"	3	102	9	135

+ Cutting dimensions followed by "+" can be cut in the size listed using the black edge of the Rotaruler 16. If you prefer an ordinary rotary ruler, cut halfway between the listed number and the next larger one-eighth inch.

PRISMS

The prisms in the chart below are proportioned with the length double the width. On the facing page are prisms three and four times as long as they are wide. Use the same cutting method shown below for all prisms on these two pages. You will need a Shapemaker 45 tool to trim two triangles off each end of the rectangle. Note that the "points" are blunted. The shape still has the appropriate ¼" seam allowance all around.

On page 74 you will find a diagonal prism in the same proportions as the 2:1 prism here. Its grain is different.

A. finished long side 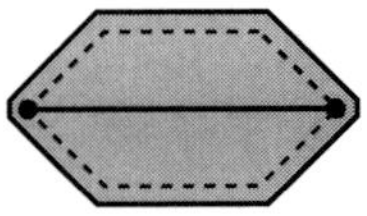   **B.** finished length 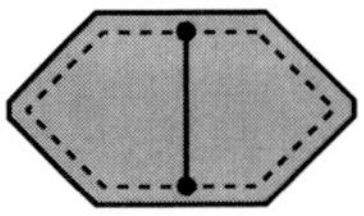   **C.** finished width

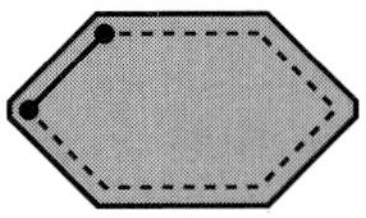

D. finished short side   straight grain 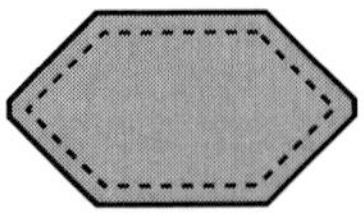   **2:1** proportions

CUTTING DIRECTIONS FOR ALL PRISMS ON PAGES 72-73

E. Find your chosen size listed in the Description columns of the chart below or on the facing page. Follow the line listing your prism size to the right for cutting directions and yield. Find Column E, the strip width. Cut a strip in the listed width, either 18" or 44" long.

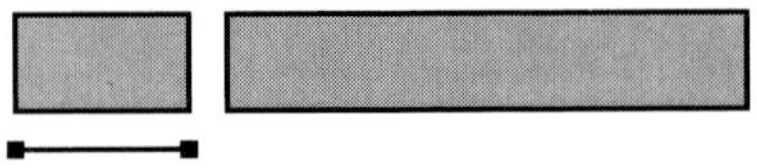

E. Cut strip width.

F. Trim a sliver off the short end at right angles to the long sides of the strip. Subcut a rectangle parallel to this end (page 14) in the size listed in Column F.

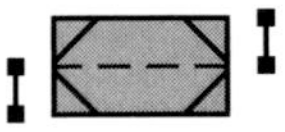

F. Subcut a rectangle.

G. Trim 2 triangles (page 15) using the Shapemaker 45 tool. Align the short line at the top of the S45 with the short end of the rectangle. Place the measurement listed in Column G over both long sides of the rectangle. Trim 2 triangles off the end of the rectangle, cutting along the S45's short sides. Repeat at the opposite end to complete a prism.

Continue cutting prisms as shown in Figure G2.

G. Trim 2 triangles from each end using the S45.

G2. Continue as shown.

#P1: PRISMS (2:1) USING SHAPEMAKER 45

Description				Cutting			Yield (Yardage)			
							18" strips		44" strips	
A. fin. long side	B. fin. prism length	C. fin. prism width	D. fin. short side	E. cut strip width	F. cut rectangle	G. mid-line to side	# per strip	# per yard	# per strip	# per yard
1¼"	2½"	1¼"	⅞"	1¾"	3"	⅞"	5	220	13	260
1⅜+	2¾+	1⅜+	1"	1⅞+	3¼+	1(-)	5	200	12	216
1½"	3"	1½"	1+	2"	3½"	1"	5	200	11	187
1¾"	3½"	1¾"	1¼"	2¼"	4"	1⅛"	4	136	10	150
2"	4"	2"	1⅜+	2½"	4½"	1¼"	3	96	8	112
2⅛"	4¼"	2⅛"	1½"	2⅝"	4¾"	1⅜(-)	3	90	8	104
2½"	5"	2½"	1¾"	3"	5½"	1½"	3	78	7	77
2¾+	5⅝+	2¾+	2"	3¼+	6⅛+	1¾(-)	2	48	6	60
3"	6"	3"	2⅛"	3½"	6½"	1¾"	2	44	6	60

+ Cutting dimensions followed by "+" can be cut in the size listed using the black edge of the Rotaruler 16. If you prefer an ordinary rotary ruler, cut halfway between the listed number and the next larger one-eighth inch.
(-) Centering dimensions followed by a "(-)" indicate that the patch should be centered with the listed ruling slightly outside the patch on both sides.

MORE PRISMS

The prisms in the chart below are proportioned with the length three times the width. Use the same general figures and cutting method shown on the facing page.

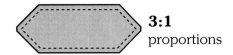

3:1
proportions

#P2: PRISMS (3:1) USING SHAPEMAKER 45

Description				Cutting			Yield (Yardage)			
							18" strips		44" strips	
A. fin. long side	B. fin. prism length	C. fin. prism width	D. fin. short side	E. cut strip width	F. cut rectangle	G. mid-line to side	# per strip	# per yard	# per strip	# per yard
2½"	3¾"	1¼"	⅞"	1¾"	4¼"	⅞"	4	176	9	180
2¾+	4¼"	1⅜+	1"	1⅞+	4¾"	1(-)	3	120	8	144
3"	4½"	1½"	1+	2"	5"	1"	3	120	8	136
3½"	5¼"	1¾"	1¼"	2¼"	5¾"	1⅛"	3	102	6	90
4"	6"	2"	1⅜+	2½"	6½"	1¼"	2	64	6	84
4¼"	6⅜"	2⅛"	1½"	2⅝"	6⅞"	1⅜(-)	2	60	5	65

+ Cutting dimensions followed by "+" can be cut in the size listed using the black edge of the Rotaruler 16. If you prefer an ordinary rotary ruler, cut halfway between the listed number and the next larger one-eighth inch.
(-) Centering dimensions followed by a "(-)" indicate that the patch should be centered with the listed ruling slightly outside the patch on both sides.

The prisms in the chart below are proportioned with the length four times the width. Use the same general figures and cutting method shown on the facing page.

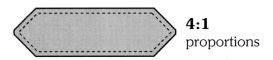

4:1
proportions

#P3: PRISMS (4:1) USING SHAPEMAKER 45

Description				Cutting			Yield (Yardage)			
							18" strips		44" strips	
A. fin. long side	B. fin. prism length	C. fin. prism width	D. fin. short side	E. cut strip width	F. cut rectangle	G. mid-line to side	# per strip	# per yard	# per strip	# per yard
3¾"	5"	1¼"	⅞"	1¾"	5½"	⅞"	3	132	7	140
4¼"	5⅝+	1⅜+	1"	1⅞+	6⅛+	1(-)	2	80	6	108
4½"	6"	1½"	1+	2"	6½"	1"	2	80	6	102
5¼"	7"	1¾"	1¼"	2¼"	7½"	1⅛"	2	68	5	75
6"	8"	2"	1⅜+	2½"	8½"	1¼"	2	64	4	56
6⅜"	8½"	2⅛"	1½"	2⅝"	9"	1⅜(-)	1	30	4	52

+ Cutting dimensions followed by "+" can be cut in the size listed using the black edge of the Rotaruler 16. If you prefer an ordinary rotary ruler, cut halfway between the listed number and the next larger one-eighth inch.
(-) Centering dimensions followed by a "(-)" indicate that the patch should be centered with the listed ruling slightly outside the patch on both sides.

DIAGONAL PRISMS

Diagonal prisms are tilted in the block. Cutting as shown puts the straight grain along the edge of the block or unit. This finished diagonal prism is proportioned with the short side half the overall height and width. The S45 method for cutting this shape is below. The regular ruler method is on the facing page.

CUTTING DIRECTIONS

D. Find your chosen size listed in the Description columns of the chart below. Follow the line listing your chosen size to the right to Column D, the strip width. Cut a strip in the listed width, either 18" or 44" long.

E. Trim a sliver off the end of the strip at a right angle to the long sides. (Right handers trim left end; left handers trim right end.) Subcut parallel (page 14) to this end at the measurement listed in Column E to make a square.

F. Use the S45 to trim a triangle (page 15) of the size listed in Column F. Align the ruling and the long side of the S45 with adjacent sides of the square and cut along the angled side of the S45 tool. Repeat at the opposite corner. This completes a diagonal prism.

Continue cutting diagonal prisms as shown in F2.

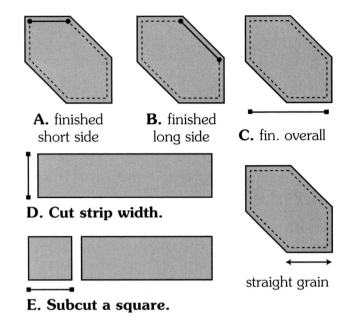

A. finished short side **B.** finished long side **C.** fin. overall

D. Cut strip width.

straight grain

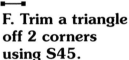

E. Subcut a square.

F. Trim a triangle off 2 corners using S45.

F2. Continue cutting this way.

#P4: DIAGONAL PRISMS USING SHAPEMAKER 45

Description			Cutting Dimensions			Yield (Yardage)			
						18" strips		44" strips	
A. fin. short side	B. fin. long side	C. fin. over-all square	D. cut strip width	E. cut square	F. cut off trian-gle	# per strip	# per yard	# per strip	# per yard
⅞"	1¼"	1¾"	2¼"	2¼"	1"	7	238	17	255
1"	1⅜+	2"	2½"	2½"	1⅛"	7	224	16	224
1¼"	1¾"	2½"	3"	3"	1⅜"	5	130	13	143
1½"	2⅛"	3"	3½"	3½"	1⅝"	5	110	11	110
1¾"	2½"	3½"	4"	4"	1⅞"	4	80	10	80
2"	2¾+	4"	4½"	4½"	2⅛"	3	48	8	56
2⅛"	3"	4¼"	4¾"	4¾"	2¼"	3	48	8	56
2½"	3½"	5"	5½"	5½"	2⅝"	3	42	7	42
3"	4¼"	6"	6½"	6½"	3⅛"	2	24	6	30
3½"	4⅞+	7"	7½"	7½"	3⅝"	2	20	5	20
3⅝"	5⅛"	7¼"	7¾"	7¾"	3¾"	2	20	5	20
4"	5⅝+	8"	8½"	8½"	4⅛"	2	16	4	16

+   For finished dimensions followed by "+," add 1/16 to the listed size.

MORE DIAGONAL PRISMS

The same diagonal prisms shown on the facing page are cut here with a regular ruler. See the description and A, B, and C figures from page 74.

D. Cut strip width.

CUTTING DIRECTIONS

D. Find your chosen size listed in the Description columns of the chart below. You may identify the diagonal prism based on either of its sides. Follow the line listing your diagonal prism size to the right for cutting directions and yield. Find Column D, the strip width. Cut a strip in the listed width, either 18" or 44" long.

E. Trim a sliver off the short end of the strip at a right angle to the long sides. (Right handers trim the left end; left handers trim the right end.) Subcut parallel (page 14) to this end at the measurement listed in Column E to make a square.

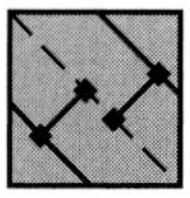

F. Subcut parallel to the diagonal (page 16). Align the measurement listed in Column F with the square's diagonal. Cut along the ruler's edge. Repeat on the opposite side of the same diagonal to complete a diagonal prism.

Continue cutting diagonal prisms as shown in Figure F2.

E. Subcut a square.

F. Cut parallel to both sides of diagonal.

F2. Continue as shown.

#P5: DIAGONAL PRISMS

Description			Cutting Dimensions			Yield (Yardage)			
						18" strips		44" strips	
A. fin. short side	B. fin. long side	C. fin. over-all square	D. cut strip width	E. cut square	F. cut dist. from diag.	# per strip	# per yard	# per strip	# per yard
⅞"	1¼"	1¾"	2¼"	2¼"	⅞"	7	238	17	255
1+	1½"	2⅛"	2⅝"	2⅝"	1"	6	180	15	195
1¼"	1¾"	2½"	3"	3"	1⅛"	5	130	13	143
1⅜+	2"	2¾+	3¼+	3¼+	1¼"	5	120	12	120
1½"	2⅛"	3"	3½"	3½"	1¼+	5	110	11	110
1¾"	2½"	3½"	4"	4"	1½"	4	80	10	80
2"	2¾+	4"	4½"	4½"	1⅝+	3	48	8	56
2⅛"	3"	4¼"	4¾"	4¾"	1¾"	3	48	8	56
2½"	3½"	5"	5½"	5½"	2"	3	42	7	42
2¾+	4"	5⅝+	6⅛+	6⅛+	2¼"	2	24	6	30
3"	4¼"	6"	6½"	6½"	2⅜"	2	24	6	30
3⅝"	5⅛"	7¼"	7¾"	7¾"	2¾+	2	20	5	20
4"	5⅝+	8"	8½"	8½"	3+	2	16	4	16

+ Cutting dimensions followed by "+" can be cut in the size listed using the black edge of the Rotaruler 16. If you prefer an ordinary rotary ruler, cut halfway between the listed number and the next larger one-eighth inch.

HALF PRISMS

The half prisms in the chart below are proportioned with the length 1½ times the width. On the facing page are prisms 2½ and 3½ times as long as they are wide. Use the same cutting method shown below for all of these half prisms. You will need a Shapemaker 45 tool to trim two triangles off one end.

Usually, I cut patches so the straight grain falls around the edge of the block. For half prisms tilted in the block, however, I get better results with the straight grain on the long side of the half prism. To avoid bias stretch, finger press until the bias is sewn.

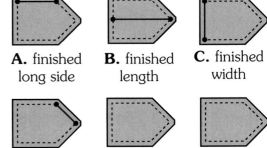

A. finished long side **B.** finished length **C.** finished width

D. finished short side   →← straight grain   **1½:1** proportions

CUTTING DIRECTIONS FOR ALL HALF PRISMS

E. Cut strip width.

E. Find your chosen size listed in the Description columns of the chart below or on the facing page. Follow the line listing your prism size to the right for cutting directions and yield. Find Column E, the strip width. Cut a strip in the listed width, either 18" or 44" long.

F. Subcut a rectangle.

F. Trim a sliver off the short end of the strip at a right angle to the long sides. (Right handers trim the left end; left handers trim the right end.) Parallel to this end, subcut (page 14) a rectangle of the size listed in Column F.

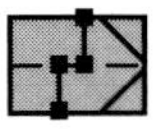

G. Trim 2 triangles from one end using the S45.

G. Trim 2 triangles (page 15) using the Shapemaker 45 tool. Align the short line at the top of the S45 with the short end of the rectangle. Place the measurement listed in Column G over both long sides of the rectangle. Trim 2 triangles off the end of the rectangle, cutting along the S45's short sides.

Continue cutting prisms as shown in Figure G2.

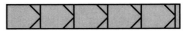

G2. Continue as shown.

#P6: HALF PRISMS (1½:1) USING SHAPEMAKER 45

Description				Cutting			Yield (Yardage)			
							18" strips		44" strips	
A. fin. long side	B. fin. prism length	C. fin. prism width	D. fin. short side	E. cut strip width	F. cut rectangle	G. mid-line to side	# per strip	# per yard	# per strip	# per yard
1¼"	1⅞"	1¼"	⅞"	1¾"	2⅜"	⅞"	7	308	16	320
1⅜+	2⅛"	1⅜+	1"	1⅞+	2⅝"	1(-)	6	240	15	270
1½"	2¼"	1½"	1+	2"	2¾"	1"	6	240	14	238
1¾"	2⅝"	1¾"	1¼"	2¼"	3⅛"	1⅛"	5	170	12	180
2"	3"	2"	1⅜+	2½"	3½"	1¼"	5	160	11	154
2⅛"	3⅛+	2⅛"	1½"	2⅝"	3⅝+	1⅜(-)	4	120	10	130

+ Cutting dimensions followed by "+" can be cut in the size listed using the black edge of the Rotaruler 16. If you prefer an ordinary rotary ruler, cut halfway between the listed number and the next larger one-eighth inch. (-) Centering dimensions followed by a "(-)" indicate that the patch should be centered with the listed ruling slightly outside the patch on both sides.

MORE HALF PRISMS

The half prisms in the chart below are proportioned with the length 2½ times the width. Use the same general figures and cutting method shown on the facing page.

2½:1 proportions

#P7: HALF PRISMS (2½:1) USING SHAPEMAKER 45

Description				Cutting			Yield (Yardage)			
							18" strips		44" strips	
A. fin. long side	B. fin. prism length	C. fin. prism width	D. fin. short side	E. cut strip width	F. cut rec-tangle	G. mid-line to side	# per strip	# per yard	# per strip	# per yard
2½"	3⅛"	1¼"	⅞"	1¾"	3⅝"	⅞"	4	176	11	220
2¾+	3½+	1⅜+	1"	1⅞+	4+	1(-)	4	160	9	162
3"	3¾"	1½"	1+	2"	4¼"	1"	4	160	9	153
3½"	4⅜"	1¾"	1¼"	2¼"	4⅞"	1⅛"	3	102	8	120
4"	5"	2"	1⅜+	2½"	5½"	1¼"	3	96	7	98
4¼"	5¼+	2⅛"	1½"	2⅝"	5¾+	1⅜(-)	3	90	6	78

+ Cutting dimensions followed by "+" can be cut in the size listed using the black edge of the Rotaruler 16. If you prefer an ordinary rotary ruler, cut halfway between the listed number and the next larger one-eighth inch.
(-) Centering dimensions followed by a "(-)" indicate that the patch should be centered with the listed ruling slightly outside the patch on both sides.

The half prisms in the chart below are proportioned with the length 3½ times the width. Use the same general figures and cutting method shown on the facing page.

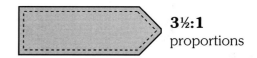

3½:1 proportions

#P8: HALF PRISMS (3½:1) USING SHAPEMAKER 45

Description				Cutting			Yield (Yardage)			
							18" strips		44" strips	
A. fin. long side	B. fin. prism length	C. fin. prism width	D. fin. short side	E. cut strip width	F. cut rec-tangle	G. mid-line to side	# per strip	# per yard	# per strip	# per yard
3¾"	4⅜"	1¼"	⅞"	1¾"	4⅞"	⅞"	3	132	8	160
4¼"	4⅞+	1⅜+	1"	1⅞+	5⅜+	1(-)	3	120	7	126
4½"	5¼"	1½"	1+	2"	5¾"	1"	3	120	6	102
5¼"	6⅛"	1¾"	1¼"	2¼"	6⅝"	1⅛"	2	68	6	90
6"	7"	2"	1⅜+	2½"	7½"	1¼"	2	64	5	70
6⅜"	7⅜+	2⅛"	1½"	2⅝"	7⅞+	1⅜(-)	2	60	5	65

+ Cutting dimensions followed by "+" can be cut in the size listed using the black edge of the Rotaruler 16. If you prefer an ordinary rotary ruler, cut halfway between the listed number and the next larger one-eighth inch.
(-) Centering dimensions followed by a "(-)" indicate that the patch should be centered with the listed ruling slightly outside the patch on both sides.

HOUSE SHAPES

The House shapes in the chart below are proportioned with the long side two times the short side. You will need a Shapemaker 45 tool to trim two triangles off one end.

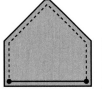 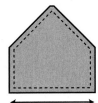

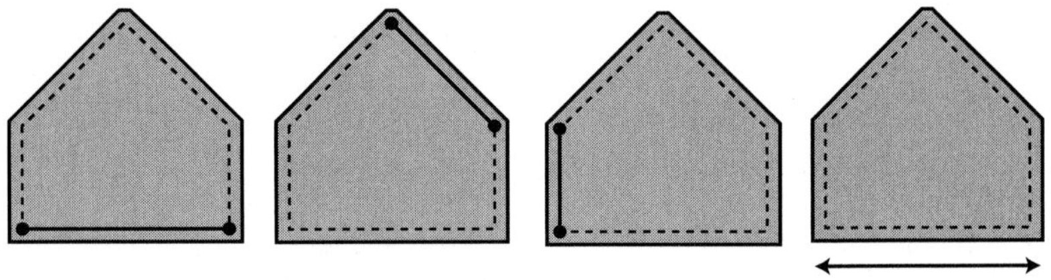

A. finished long side   **B.** finished med. side   **C.** finished short side   straight grain

CUTTING DIRECTIONS

D. Find your chosen size listed in the Description columns of the chart below. Follow the line listing your House size to the right to Column D, the strip width. Cut a strip in the listed width, either 18" or 44" long.

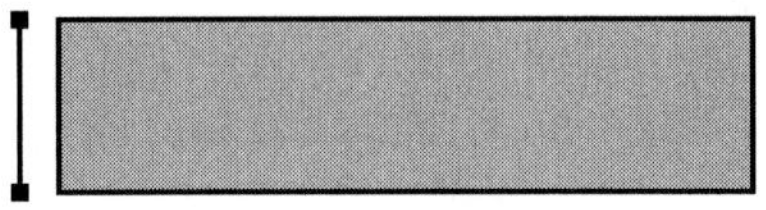

E. Trim a sliver off the short end of the strip at a right angle to the long sides. (Right handers trim the left end; left handers trim the right end.) Parallel to this end, subcut (page 14) a square of the size listed in Column E.

F. Trim 2 triangles (page 15) using the S45 tool. Align the short line at the top of the S45 with the top of the square. Place the measurement listed in Column F over two opposite sides of the square. Trim 2 triangles off the top of the square, cutting along the S45's short sides.

Continue cutting House shapes as shown in Figure F2.

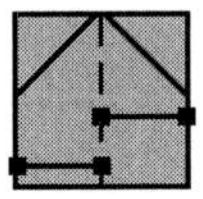

D. Cut strip width.

E. Subcut a square.

F2. Continue as shown.

F. Trim 2 triangles from the top using the S45.

#P9: HOUSE SHAPES USING SHAPEMAKER 45

Description			Cutting			Yield (Yardage)			
						18" strips		44" strips	
A. fin. long side	B. fin. med. side	C. fin. short side	D. cut strip width	E. cut square	F. dist. from mid-line to side	# per strip	# per yard	# per strip	# per yard
1¾"	1¼"	⅞"	2¼"	2¼"	1⅛"	7	238	17	255
2"	1⅜+	1"	2½"	2½"	1¼"	7	224	16	224
2⅛"	1½"	1+	2⅝"	2⅝"	1⅜(-)	6	180	15	195
2½"	1¾"	1¼"	3"	3"	1½"	5	130	13	143
3"	2⅛"	1½"	3½"	3½"	1¾"	5	110	11	110
3½"	2½"	1¾"	4"	4"	2"	4	80	10	80
4"	2¾+	2"	4½"	4½"	2¼"	3	48	8	56
4¼"	3"	2⅛"	4¾"	4¾"	2⅜"	3	48	8	56
5"	3½"	2½"	5½"	5½"	2¾"	3	42	7	42
6"	4¼"	3"	6½"	6½"	3¼"	2	24	6	30

+   For finished dimensions followed by a "+," add ¹⁄₁₆" to the listed number.
(-)   Centering dimensions followed by a "(-)" indicate that the patch should be centered with the listed ruling slightly outside the patch on both sides.

Resources

ROTARY CUTTING TOOLS

Look for the following recommended products at your favorite quilting supply retailer:

Judy Martin's Ultimate Rotary Tools

Crosley-Griffith, 1321 Broad Street, Grinnell, IA 50112
R16: Rotaruler 16, 7" x 19" ruler with sixteenths
PT: Point Trimmer, helps align patches for piecing
S45: Shapemaker 45, versatile triangle tool and more

Patched Works, Inc.

13330 Watertown Plank Road, Elm Grove, WI 53122
Rotary Rule: 3½" x 24" ruler in white or black
Big Mama: 6½" x 12" ruler in white or black
Rotary Mate: 3½" x 12" ruler with speedies, white or black

Quilter's Rule™

817 Mohr Avenue, Waterford, WI 53185
QR-1: 6½" x 24" ruler with gripping action
QR-JR: 4½" x 14" ruler with gripping action
QR-Ms: 6½" x 6½" ruler with gripping action
QR-T6 or QR-T12: triangle ruler with gripping action
rotary cutter: with positive-locking shield

Master Piece® Products

10481 N.W. 107th Avenue, Granger, IA 50109
Master Piece® 45: 8" x 24" ruler with ⅛" grid
Master Piece® Static Stickers: acetate for use with rulers

Omnigrid®

18G: 3" x 18" ruler with ⅛" grid
4G or 6G: small square with ⅛" grid
96 or 96L: half-square triangle tool
98 or 98L: quarter-square triangle tool
15: big square ruler, 15" x 15"
Omnimats: one side green, one side gray

Olfa® Corporation

P.O. Box 747, Plattsburgh, NY 12901
RTY-3/G: 60mm rotary cutter
RTY-2/G: 45mm rotary cutter
RTY-1/G: 28mm rotary cutter
RB60: 60mm replacement blade
RB45: 45mm replacement blade
RB28: 28mm replacement blade
RM-MG: 35" x 23" rotary mat, green

Fiskars®

7811 West Stewart Ave., Wausau, WI 54401
Softouch®: rotary cutter convertible for 45mm and 65mm

CM Designs

507 Staudaher, Bozeman, MT 59715
Add-A-Quarter™, 6" or 12": for rotary cuttting odd shapes

Clearview Triangle™

8311 - 180th St. S.E., Snohomish, WA 98296
1: 60° triangle tool, up to 6"
2: 60° triangle tool, up to 12"
3: 60° triangle tool, up to 8"
4: 30°-120° half diamond tool

EZ Quilting by Wrights®

85 South Street, West Warren, MA 01092
8823753: Tri-Recs Tools™: cuts "tri" & "recs" triangles

From Marti Michell™

P.O. Box 80218, Atlanta, GA 30366
8641 or 8642: Kaleido-Ruler™: cuts Kaleidoscope patches

MAIL-ORDER CATALOGUES

If you don't find what you want locally, try one of these mail-order sources or contact the manufacturer:

Clotilde, Inc.

1-800-772-2891

Connecting Threads

P.O. Box 8940, Vancouver, WA 98668-8940
1-800-574-6454

Keepsake Quilting

Rte. 25B, P.O. Box 1618, Centre Harbor, NH 03226
1-800-865-9458

The Quilt Farm

P.O. Box 7877, St. Paul, MN 55107
1-800-435-6201

Quilts & Other Comforts

1 Quilters Lane, Box 4100, Golden CO 80402-4100
1-800-881-6624

OTHER JUDY MARTIN PRODUCTS

Crosley-Griffith, 1321 Broad Street, Grinnell, IA 50112

Patterns

Judy's Fancy
Grandma's Porch

Books

The Block Book (publication date: 1998)
Pieced Borders, coauthored by Marsha McCloskey
Yes You Can! Make Stunning Quilts from Simple Patterns

Cover Photos

The quilt blocks on the cover are from *The Block Book*.

INDEX TO CHARTS

INDEX TO TOPICS